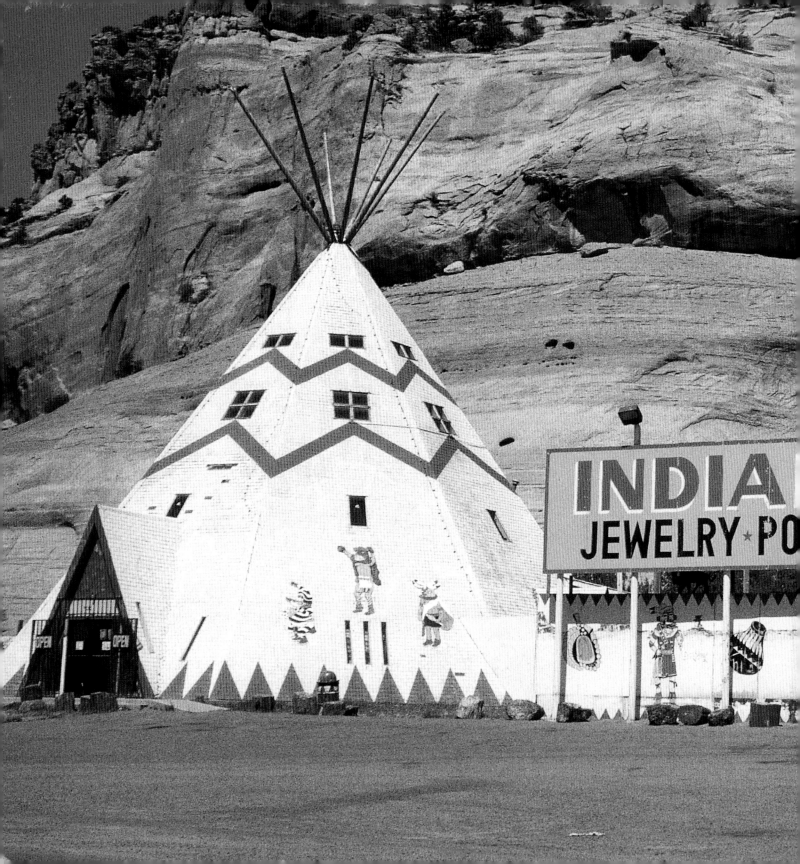

Route 66

LIVES ON THE ROAD

Jon Robinson

MBI Publishing Company

First published in 2001 by MBI Publishing Company,
729 Prospect Avenue, PO Box 1, Osceola, WI
54020-0001 USA

MBI Publishing Company books are also available at discounts in
bulk quantity for industrial or sales-promotional use. For details
write to Special Sales Manager at Motorbooks International
Wholesalers & Distributors, 729 Prospect Avenue, PO Box 1,
Osceola, WI 54020-0001 USA.

Library of Congress Catalog-in-Publication Data
Robinson, Jon G.,
   Route 66: lives on the road / Jon G. Robinson.
        p. cm.—(nostalgic treasures)
   Includes index.
   ISBN 0-7603-0766-0 (hc. : alk. paper)
    1. United States Highway 66—Collectibles—Automobile
Travel—West (U.S.)–History. I. Title.
   NK808 .R56 2001
   388.1'0978'075–dc21.22'12'075—dc21   00-063832

On the front cover: Some of the friendly faces who give life to
Route 66. From left are Pat Matlach of Desert Motors in
Victorville, California; Becky Ransom, a sixth-grade history teacher
in Amarillo, Texas; Dave Pouquette of the Route 66 Place and
Twisters in Williams, Arizona; Bill Shea of Shea's service station
in Springfield, Illinois; and posing in front of the Blue Swallow
Motel are David and Chris Williams. The two operate
www.route66.com in Atlanta, Georgia.

On the frontispiece: An authentic road marker bearing the
famous Route 66 shield.

On the title page: Route 66 is full of roadside icons, from
famous motels and cafes to gas stations and tourists traps. This
Indian Arts & Crafts store beckons motorists to stop in for a break
on their long trip through the desert.

On the back cover: Of all the signs posted along Route 66,
the signs for the Jack Rabbit Trading Post and The Big Texan are
arguably the most famous.

Edited by Keith Mathiowetz
Designed by Tom Heffron

Printed in China

CONTENTS

DEDICATION

To a faithful friend who's carried me thousands of miles on Route 66 and many other great American highways. The real thing.

ACKNOWLEDGMENTS

Contributing photography: Shellee Graham, Marc Mirabile, Scott Piotrowski.

Copyrighted material: Brown and Bigelow, St. Paul, Minnesota, "Hilda" calendars; TV Guide, *TV Guide* covers; C. A. Stevens, Summit Inn, Hesperia, California; Cheryl Cobb, Missouri State Highway Patrol, Jefferson City, Missouri; Scott Piotrowski, 66 Productions, Angel Delgadillo's quotes from film *158 Miles to Yesterday.*

Featured artwork: Duane Bryers, artist, "Hilda," Sonoita, Arizona; Dawne Holmes, artist, "Kicking Back on Route 66"; Jerry McClanahan, artist, "El Vado Motel," "Standard Station, Sayer, OK," "Route 66 Art Cards"; Jim Ross, Ghost Town Press, "Here It Is! Route 66 Map Set"; Ken Turmel, artist, "Route 66 and More . . ."; Bob Waldmire, artist, "Map of Old Route 66," "Missouri," "Oklahoma," "Texas," "Arizona," "Tee Pee Curios" postcards.

Sincere thanks to Dan Harlow, *Route 66 West;* Paul Taylor, *Route 66 Magazine;* Sally Noe, Gallup, New Mexico; Southwest Indian Foundation Cultural Center, Gallup, New Mexico; Becky Ransom, Amarillo, Texas; Delbert Trew, Devil's Rope Museum, McLean, Texas; John Hill and Heather Roulet, Oklahoma Route 66 Museum, Clinton, Oklahoma; Pat Baker, Elk City, Oklahoma; Michael Wallis, Tulsa, Oklahoma; Jim Gilbert, Friends of the Old Chain of Rocks Bridge, St. Louis, Missouri; Tom Teague, Route 66 Hall of Fame, McLean, Illinois; Jim Hinckley, Kingman, Arizona; and Linda Morrel, Sage College, Albany, New York.

Special thanks to Scott and Susan Nassif and the whole crew of NAPA Auto Parts, Apple Valley, California.

—Jon Robinson

Sunset at the restored McLean, Texas, Phillips 66 gas station.
Scott Piotrowski

INTRODUCTION

Juan and Angel Delgadillo.

What started out as a history of Route 66 quickly became a scrapbook of people, memories, collectibles, and passions for a very special stretch of pavement. Route 66 wasn't like any other road. It transcended being a two-lane ribbon of tar to become an international symbol of freedom and dreams. Indeed, many people took to the road to find their riches at the other end. Many others helped those who were traveling by working along the highway, serving up meals, pumping gas, and operating motels, among other activities. Still others used the road for vacation purposes, driving to California, the Grand Canyon, and the deserts of the Southwest. In the end, it is the culmination of all these people's experiences, and not just the road, that make Route 66 a legend and a subject of endless fascination.

THE ROAD

Think of the difficulty of selling cars in the first few decades of the twentieth century. An automobile cost as much as a house, and in those hurly-burly days, the debate as to what would be the prominent fuel threatened to make a driver's expensive purchase instantly obsolete. Worst of all, once the car was purchased, the only roads to drive it on were muddy, rutted wagon roads.

Freedom is what motivated early drivers—choice and control. While the United States had been crisscrossed by an efficient and affordable railroad system, one still gave up a lot of control to the railroad's destination list and schedule. The automobile's scent of freedom made the high cost, fuel difficulties, and bad roads worthwhile.

The importance of good roads was reaching a critical point in those early years. North of Los Angeles, California, is a forbidding wall of rock and sand formed by the intersection of the San Gabriel, Sierra Madre, and Tehachapi mountain ranges. Not just high and steep, these mountains are broad. So impenetrable was this wall that California was very nearly split into two states—North California and South California. What broke the barrier and kept the Golden State whole was a 20-foot-wide strip of concrete that wound violently through the mountains, partly teetering atop a ridge line and partly crawling through a canyon. It was built in 1915 and called the Ridge Route.

Very little is said about it today, but the nation must have been watching the Ridge Route, among others, as it saved a state. The year 1916 brought the Federal Aid Road Act, which gave the States federal funds for road construction. In 1921 the mechanism refined itself into the Federal Highway Act, which required that each state designate 7 percent of its highways under the federal system. The stage was set for the mother of all highways.

Oklahoma businessman Cyrus Avery rightfully gets the lion's share of credit for making Route 66 a reality. Individual states had long since established highway associations concerned with choosing paths and raising funds for construction. The Associated Highway Associations of America elected Cyrus Avery as its president in 1921. In the same period, Avery became head of the American Association of State Highway Officials, the 1924 annual meeting of which produced a request to the Department of Agriculture that resulted in the formation of various public boards and federal departments whose task it was to lay out the U.S. highway system, initially, by connecting existing state highways and established wagon roads.

Fights were common between communities as each vied for a major highway to come down its main street. According to John Hill, former director of the Oklahoma Route 66 Museum, each of these communities could easily remember only 30 and 40 years before when the railroads had passed through some towns and bypassed others. The towns with

Collecting the relics of Route 66 may be a sign that America's throwaway habits are being given second thoughts as people remember and miss the old things of the past.

rails prospered, and the towns without dried up and blew away. The fights for highways were matters of life and death, and decades later as the towns that got the U.S. highways were bypassed by the interstate highway system, the dependence on the old highways was graphically illustrated.

One path was drawn connecting Chicago, St. Louis, Oklahoma City, Albuquerque, and Los Angeles—encompassing Illinois, Missouri, one corner of Kansas, Oklahoma, the Texas Panhandle, New Mexico, Arizona, and California. U.S. Highway 66 was dedicated on November 11, 1926.

Improvements came fast. The saw-tooth-shaped route through Illinois was bypassed in the early 1930s by a parallel straight line to the east. The wildly serpentine route through Santa Fe and Albuquerque was bypassed in the late 1930s, shortening the distance by more than 80 miles and bypassing the nightmarish La Bajada Hill and its 18 deadly switchback curves. Route 66 merged with U.S. 395 and U.S. 91 to negotiate California's treacherous Cajon Pass, and the path down the gorge was an ever changing work-in-progress from the early days of wagon roads until the final form of Interstate 15 circa 1970—encompassing all of Route 66's historic era.

HUMAN DRAMA

Route 66's heaviest dramas did not concern concrete and asphalt. They were not carved into public memory and imagination by bulldozers and dynamite. Route 66's most sensational dramas were all too human.

A lonely 1952 Oldsmobile 98 in Shamrock, Texas, looks to Route 66 for its next owner. Once an elegant, high-quality road machine, it may owe its survival to being spotted by a Route 66 devotee who wants to see the road through the windshield of the real thing.

Author Michael Wallis chronicled the nefarious career of armed robber Pretty Boy Floyd and the criminal's preference for speedy, well-paved Route 66 as his escape path of choice through Missouri and Oklahoma in the late 1920s and early 1930s.

The stock market crash of 1929 was bad enough for the rural farmers of Oklahoma, but when compounded with the horrendous drought and the Dust Bowl it created, starvation and fleeing refugees became a reality in America. Route 66 was their highway. It was a highway to promised work and a new life in the Golden State. John Steinbeck's dramatization of this circumstance was the *Grapes of Wrath* in which he dubbed Route 66 the "Mother Road."

The 1940s saw the world at war—a gigantic war that claimed the lives of tens-of-millions, destroyed entire nations, and gave subsequent generations names that personify absolute, unspeakable evil. The magnificent effort to stop the evil was partly played out on Route 66 as millions of troops traversed the American continent en masse to gather where they were needed. General George S. Patton, "Old Blood and Guts," personally escorted his famed tank divisions on practice maneuvers through California's Mojave Desert with Route 66 as their main artery of travel.

With the end of the world's greatest war so far, Americans settled into the tranquil rhythms of postwar prosperity, and by the early 1950s the eight-cylinder engine and the family vacation were the orders of the day. The children of that time have grown to be some of Route 66's most devoted nostalgists as they remember their intact families enjoying summer swims at Missouri's Lake of the Ozarks, their rattlesnake souvenirs from the Texas Panhandle, their rubber tomahawks and toy Indian headdresses from New Mexico, and the stunning visions of Arizona's Painted Desert and Grand Canyon, along with California's "Hollywood" sign and the Pacific Ocean. All of these things were seen through the windshield of the big, comfortable, high-quality American car Dad guided down the highway as Mom sang along with the radio playing "Tennessee Waltz."

The 1950s also showed America that two-lane Route 66 was not enough, and visions of multilane, limited-access superhighways were dancing in the heads of government officials, the trucking industry, and the car-buying public who by then had had enough of driving 200-horsepower cars stuck behind trucks at 35 miles per hour. President Eisenhower signed the interstate highway system into existence, and the writing was on the wall for Route 66.

As bypasses accelerated through the 1960s, a new human drama took place as once-thriving towns died quick, horrible deaths. Chains of lock step motels and fast food joints took the places of the individually owned businesses that gave Route 66 its never-anything-the-same-way-twice character. The petroleum crisis of the early 1970s was the final blow to the independently owned gas stations. By the late 1970s, successful business owners were reduced to employees, and individuality was gone. It was no one's fault. Those were the times.

NOSTALGIA

The memories, however, were much harder to kill, and by the middle of the 1980s people were grumbling. They missed the America of their youth and began to take small steps toward finding it again. They started taking trips, taking photos, and picking up fragments. Tom Teague wrote *Searching for 66*, Tom Snyder guided people down the highway with his *Route 66 Traveler's Guide*, and Michael Wallis made the whole road come to life with his Pulitzer Prize–nominated *Route 66—The Mother Road*. A progression of successful books and videos followed, extending this strip of road all around the world.

Nostalgists began asking themselves about the old sign Grandpa has in his garage, where they put that rubber tomahawk, what Route 66 postcards were at the swap meet this week, what old maps are still in the glovebox of Dad's DeSoto, where there might be a piece of broken pavement. . . . The collecting began in earnest in the early 1990s, and realizing some items are rare and special, museums opened with the goal of showing the few pieces to thousands of people. The memories of forgotten people have become valuable tools for the historians of the Oklahoma Historical Society and others, and their recorded oral histories will live forever. The last and best news is that in a small way, Route 66's roadside has come alive again with souvenirs for the tourist, and successful gift shops and their campy items are well in keeping with the road's always-commercial shoulders.

From the 1920s to the twenty-first century, from serious fragments of history to comical tourist souvenirs, from the valuable antiques of long ago to modern antenna balls, from chunks of concrete to human memories, they are all the gems of Route 66.

Gas pumps and signs adorn the interior of the Oklahoma Route 66 Museum.

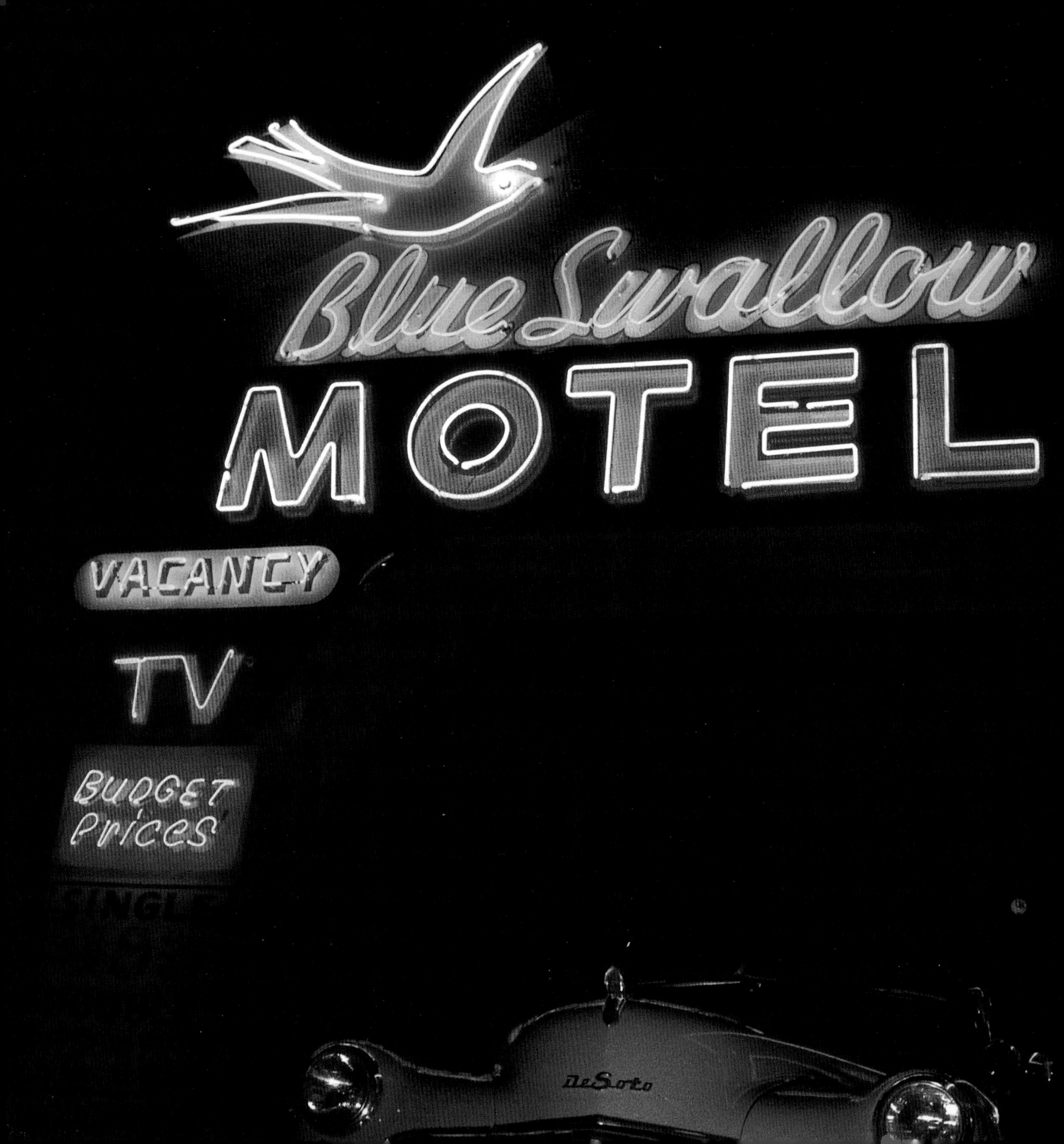
Blue Swallow
MOTEL
VACANCY
TV
BUDGET
Prices
DeSoto

CHAPTER 1

Gas, Food, and Lodging

Some automotive historians claim that for a time in the early twentieth century, it was easier for a motorist on the East Coast to find a place to get his electric car's batteries charged than it was to find fuel for his gasoline- or kerosene-powered road machine. A debate raged for some time as to whether electric or fuel cars would be the standard of the automotive world. As roads spread out from the cities, however, fuel-burning cars won out because the driver didn't need to stand around for an hour during a long trip waiting for batteries to charge.

It wasn't long before the driver and passengers needed fueling as well, and the eye-catching, affordable, quick-meal diner became a roadside fixture—eventually minting the words *fast food*.

A fond memory for many older Americans is the safety of sleeping on little beds built off the running boards of their cars with rarely a thought to crime or danger. For others, unpleasant weather, changing times, and a more modern world led them to warm, clean beds inside roadside motels any time the sandman struck.

Route 66 is a long, long road with thousands of stories generated by the venerable fixtures of gas, food, and lodging—from Phillips 66's use of its most profitable road in its name to the griffins, Indians, and athletic symbols of other fuel companies; from the Snow Cap's comedian owner in the West to the Cozy Dog's perfection of corndog technology in the East; from the elegant glass brick, neon, and swimming pools of urban lodges to the tiny rooms, cold water, and frigid adobe of the rural motels.

While gas stations, restaurants, and motels are not unique to Route 66, the ones occupying the Chicago-to-L.A. roadside were among the most successful anywhere.

The bright neon of the Blue Swallow Motel in Tucumcari, New Mexico, pierces the night's darkness to attract motorists on Route 66. The motel is a landmark along the Mother Road.

Relics of gassing up on the Mother Road at Shea's retired station in Springfield, Illinois.

For past travelers they hold some of their most vivid memories. There was stiff competition among them for the traveler's dollar bill, and their blazing colors, neon flicker, and imaginative promotions were all designed to make the driver pass the business next door and drop those dollars at the winning visual shout.

The men and women who ran—and continue to run—these establishments are the genuine treasures of Route 66. To them the old road wasn't just a way to make

a living but a way of life. The following profiles spotlight a few typical people who made Route 66 their home and business. Their stories, memories, and collections of Route 66–related objects keep the Mother Road alive.

BILL SHEA— THE GASOLINE MAN OF SPRINGFIELD, ILLINOIS

"Most of my life—especially my working life—was spent in this city block," says Bill Shea of his 50-year career spent between 11th Street and Percy Avenue, on Springfield's section of Route 66 known as Peoria Avenue.

With the end of Route 66, the beginning of another business, and the resurgence of 66 interest, Shea has managed to persist through the decades and semiretire into one of the most complete gas station memorabilia collections exhibited on Route 66—with the added touch that much of the equipment in Shea's collection was actually in daily use in his station through the Mother Road's heyday.

Moise Deruy was known for going by the nickname Mud and owning a Texaco station at the corner of Peoria Avenue and 11th Street through the 1930s, and for a time 66 travelers were greeted by a sign on the station that read "Mud's Tire Repair."

Like a lot of young men in prewar America, Shea hung around a service station picking up a few bucks and soaking up the gas-and-cars atmosphere.

The bombing of Pearl Harbor sent a 20-year-old Shea into the army, and upon his return, postwar prosperity handed Shea the opportunity to buy into the business in 1946, making the station Deruy and Shea Texaco. Within months of the partnership's founding, Deruy died, leaving Shea the sole owner.

After nine-and-a-half years in the modest station, Shea closed one evening at the south end of the block and opened the next morning at the north end of the same block at the corner of Peoria and Percy Avenues in a brand-new corporate-owned Marathon gas station with two indoor bays and all the latest equipment. Yet he still remembers fondly the style of business that took place in the modest Texaco station.

"People might think, my god, how did people get anything done in a gas station like that," Shea recalls, "but a station was actually the center of information for everybody. When people would come into a station, and [the attendant] would tell them directions, he would

"Most of my life—especially my working life—was spent in this city block," says Bill Shea of his 50-year career spent between Eleventh Street and Percy Avenue on the Springfield, Illinois, section of Route 66 known as Peoria Avenue.

always say, 'Go to the hard road, and turn right or turn left.' Sixty-six was always referred to as the hard road. The cops we had then were never called policemen. The state policemen were called hard road cops. It's a language of its own on 66."

Shea added truck shells and boats to his list of products in the late 1960s. With the gas crunch of 1974 and Peoria Avenue's conversion from 66 to Interstate 55 Business in 1977, Shea found the gasoline business actually interfering with the truck top biz. He stopped selling gasoline in 1982, but the story hardly ends here.

The doldrums of the 1970s and 1980s were as potentially cruel to Shea as anyone else along 66, but

Cans from the past. Sixty-six travelers will remember the days when a gas station attendant checked a driver's oil, belts, hoses, and tires.

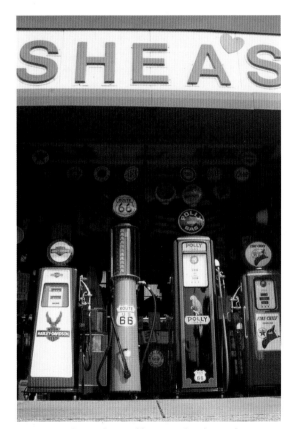

Pop art and genuine artifacts at Shea's: Harley-Davidson and Route 66 adorn two pumps in an artsy statement. The mammoth black-and-green Pollygas pump was a fixture of the Wilshire Oil Company of Los Angeles, and Texaco's "Firechief" is wearing its alarming fire engine red.

Oil cans were metal in prewar America, but after Pearl Harbor metal production was diverted to the war effort. Oil cans were replaced temporarily with glass quart bottles. These examples from Pennzoil are rare commodities because it was a common practice for a gas station attendant to smash the bottles to save room in trash cans. Few survive, but they can still be seen at Shea's.

On Route 66 near Vega, Texas.

Most likely a victim of the gas crunch, this formerly independent gas station is being taken back by nature on the banks of Route 66 near Lebanon, Missouri.

Shea had an idea. He started showing a collection of gas station equipment to a world that he sensed was getting a bit nostalgic for the era that made up the bulk of his career.

Outside and immediately inside, the station is highlighted by looming, bigger-than-life gas pumps from other times. The brightly colored, prewar Shell and Texaco visible pumps outside and varieties of electric pumps inside are dominated by the mammoth black-and-green Polly Gas pump from the 1940s with its detailed green parrot who seems ready to say, "Sorry about the rationing, pal."

It's the little things in Shea's collection that say the most about Route 66, however. Wearing his 1950s-vintage Texaco hat that makes one want to sing "We're the men of Texaco . . ." and catch an episode of *The Milton Berle Show*, Shea begins to tell the tales.

"Some of this stuff I've had for over 50 years like that wringer, the first ledger I ever kept, a money changer [for the attendant's belt], and that adding machine," he says.

Photos from the 1940s show a rag wringer on the island of Shea's Texaco station. The wringer hangs from the rafters with coats of new paint, and this simple device is an education in itself when a guy like Shea is there to fill in the blanks.

"We kept [the wringer] right on the island, and we kept a chamois in there," he explains. "It has a little trough for the water to go back down into the bucket. You see, nowadays, we have these little, rough, nylon sponges to clean the bugs off the windshield, but we used corncobs back then. We would put corncobs in the water and just leave them in the bucket."

When finished scrubbing off bugs with the corncobs, the attendant would wipe the windshield down with the chamois and wring it out for another use.

When it came time to pull a favorite oil can from his ample collection, Shea immediately chose a Havoline can from the 1930s.

"This Havoline can says it was produced by the Indian Refining Company. Texaco wanted the Havoline oil and Indian wouldn't sell it to them, so Texaco bought the refinery to get the oil," Shea says. "Indian Oil Company was based in Lawrenceville, Illinois." Shea's affection for this company is enhanced by his Indian Refining Company sign with a 1927 date on the back.

Phillips 66 oil cans and a promotional at the Devil's Rope Museum in McLean, Texas.

World War II put a strain on the nation, and on the cars. There was no metal available for conveniences like motor oil cans—thus, Shea's collection of brown glass Pennzoil bottles, which are extremely rare because gas station attendants smashed the bottles to save space in the trash barrels.

What was Shea's pre-1955 Texaco station like? A visitor only needs to look at a scale model of Shea's to see. The artist who made the model took a magnified look at photos of the station and re-created it right down to the number of bricks in the pillars. Shea's post-1955 Marathon station is itself a full-scale model of petroleum nostalgia.

A tangle of signs, equipment, hats, uniforms, and Route 66 shields hang from the rafters and from the walls around the office—a pleasant tangle that keeps the visitor looking for remembered objects from childhood.

While most of these objects can be seen in quality collections of gas station memorabilia, Shea's are special and relevant to the 66 enthusiast. Oil cans are not exclusive to Route 66, but *these* are. Gas pumps aren't exclusive to Route 66, but *these* are. Oil company signs aren't exclusive to Route 66, but *these* are. Shea's building and many of these objects faced Route 66 throughout their working years, making them the real McCoy.

"I've been real fortunate," Shea says. "Some people went completely out of business when the interstate bypassed them, and some of those buildings are empty to this day. All along through the whole country, the small family businesses were on quicksand—going down and down. Now, Route 66 is a part of my whole life, and I'm a part of it. There are few people who have spent as much continuous time on Route 66 as I have. I've been here since my life started, and I'll probably be here 'til I die."

A Phillips 66 pump-top globe dominates a display case at the Old Route 66 Emporium in Staunton, Illinois.

Phillips 66 fragments in the Michael Wallis collection.

The refueling canopy of
the famous U-Drop Inn
in Shamrock, Texas.

One of the places that sparked the modern Route 66 nostalgia movement—the Snow Cap in Seligman, Arizona.

JUAN DELGADILLO'S
SNOW CAP DRIVE-IN—
SELIGMAN, ARIZONA

It's a gamble. The front door of this little burger joint has two doorknobs, one of which will actually open the door while the other will just leave the would-be entrant feeling foolish for picking the wrong one. Between the knobs is a sign saying, "Sorry, we're open." Above it all are signs stating proudly that the little eatery serves "Dead Chicken." Spinning the wheel of fate, a knob is picked, the door is opened, and a hungry traveler leaves the twenty-first century and re-enters the 1950s.

Finally filled with the aroma of good, old-fashioned fast food, travelers are eager to order food and eat, but there's a trial first. The owner asks the customers if they would like new straws and napkins or used ones at a discount. A mustard bottle squirts a yellow string at the customers. The owner asks if they wants cheese on their cheeseburgers.

It's no fun to be taunted and delayed when hungry from traveling, right? Separating this experience from any other is the fact that the travelers came all the way to Seligman, Arizona, specifically to get a full dose of this wackiness from Snow Cap Drive-In owner Juan Delgadillo and to take in the sights and sounds of the original period equipment, signs, and advertisements that Juan has gathered over the course of five decades.

Juan and his brother, Angel, have been Seligman fixtures since growing up there in the 1920s and 1930s. The sons of the town barber, the brothers chose different paths but remained loyal to their little town. Angel followed his father's career, but put a popular pool hall behind his barber shop. Juan went to work for the Santa Fe Railroad, which had a large engine and track repair facility in the now-empty fields on the south side of town.

Juan had worked for Santa Fe for more than 20 years when it became clear that a change was in the wind. Diesel was quickly replacing steam on the Santa Fe rails before and after World War II, and layoffs were sure to come as the rail facilities in Seligman began cutting back operations. As savings would allow, Juan began

The wacky one himself, Snow Cap owner Juan Delgadillo. With a straight face, his "full treatment" makes for laughs and memories as his jokes attack customers faster than a Rocket 88 on Route 66.

stockpiling lumber, and when his life was finally bitten by the railroad layoffs in 1952, he was ready to build his burger joint on the shoulder of one of the busiest highways in America. At more than 5,000 feet elevation, Seligman's surrounding prairie can be a cold place in the winter, and snow can linger on the mountains to the east very late into the spring. The Snow Cap name fits well, and Juan Delgadillo's personality and humor fit Route 66's campy side well.

For the Route 66 enthusiast, the Snow Cap is a chance to see old equipment still in use. From the 1950s-vintage icecream machine and cash register to the Coca-Cola ads on the walls, the Snow Cap is the real thing.

Juan is also the real thing, and his character and wit make for quite an experience—one that makes you want to share it with everyone you know. It's not unusual during a leisurely visit on the Snow Cap patio to watch carload after carload of 66 tourists approach the front door under the direction of one person who has experienced the Snow Cap before. Once a 66 enthusiast has received a full treatment from Juan, it's only natural to bring friends and family for a dose. People seek common experiences to feel closer to each other, and years after the fact, shared experiences like the Snow Cap can bring smiles to faces of people who have the same memories.

Angel Delgadillo is recognized as one of the founding fathers of the modern Route 66 nostalgia movement, having helped make Arizona's portion of Route 66 a state historical monument and having turned his barber shop into a small Route 66 museum and gift shop. Juan's contribution has been good cheer, good food, and a jumbled collection of burger joint trappings like no other. Other campy 66-side relics like the Regal Reptile Ranch in Texas or the Blue Whale in Oklahoma are either gone or out of operation, but at the Snow Cap, a piece of this humorous, self-aware culture can still be absorbed. Fortunately for all Route 66 devotees, the Snow Cap seems confident to live on for some time. Juan's sons, John and Robert, have learned the shtick well, and potentially, Juan's presence may be felt for decades to come.

Artist Dawne Holmes, a Harley-Davidson specialist, poses with one of her works, "Kicking Back on Route 66," and its subject, the Snow Cap.

The Summit Inn's 1952 gas station at the top of California's Cajon Pass adorned with fuel symbols of the past.

THE SUMMIT INN—
CAJON PASS, CALIFORNIA

California's Cajon Pass today is still not the most hospitable place in America. Even as Interstate 15 straightened, widened, and leveled the worst of Route 66's old path over the hill, the improvements have done nothing to make the climb cooler in the summer or warmer in the winter.

Route 66 took travelers east and north out of the fertile valleys of San Bernardino and Los Angeles and into the hot and sometimes harsh Mojave Desert. The barrier between the two climates are the San Gabriel and San Bernardino Mountains. California's famous San Andreas earthquake fault has put a giant crack in the ground between the two mountain ranges—thus, creating what has been one of the busiest mountain passes in America for more than 100 years and one of the best places anywhere to serve the beleaguered traveler. The Summit Inn, in both its 1930s and 1950s incarnations, has served that need.

Entering from the south and heading for the desert, the Cajon Pass is about 10 miles of climbing and winding road. On today's Interstate 15, it takes about 15 minutes to traverse the gorge and crest the high Cajon Summit and begin the gentle fall into the Mojave. On winding, twisting, sheer-drop Route 66, it was not unusual for this drive to take more than three hours. Temperamental weather could easily double that figure.

In summer, 100-degree temperatures made the climb on 66 unbearable and damaging to cars as they overheated. In winter, blowing snow and freezing temperatures made a long trip longer and scarier. In either circumstance, Route 66 was nearly impossible to stop on, with narrow shoulders and steep drops. If any car or truck did stop, so did anyone else for miles behind, making a parking lot out of the two-lane. The nature of the road forced the motorist or the trucker all the way to the top before they were able to finally stop safely.

In summer, the Summit Inn was a much needed water stop, serving ice water and ice cream to heat-tortured travelers. In winter, the original Summit Inn's big, stone fireplace was a cozy, welcoming sight.

Changing alignments of the highway eventually forced the Summit Inn to move about a half-mile in 1952. The original Cajon Summit sits between the separated north- and southbound lanes of I-15 at the top of the Cajon Pass high above the heads of today's interstate drivers.

The initial location of the Summit Inn on Route 66's original path over the Cajon Pass Summit. This site now sits empty high on a peak between the separated north- and southbound lanes of Interstate 15. *Summit Inn collection*

A Summit Inn postcard of an antique automobile club meet at the Summit in 1953. The cars that were new then are now themselves antiques. *Summit Inn collection*

The venerable interior of the Summit Inn with many authentic artifacts on display.

While the 1952 building is not the original Summit Inn, it still boasts great highway-side atmosphere, a historic place along 66, a collection of authentic period pieces, and the personalities of its long-time owner and even longer-time manager.

Approaching the Summit Inn, a 66 cruiser may be disappointed to see the two modern gas stations obstructing the view of the restaurant, but with a curve into the parking lot, the original 1952 gas station and restaurant come into full view with Interstate 15 virtually out of sight. On the south side of the restaurant is the now-unused motel portion of the complex, showing that the Summit Inn did for many years encompass all that makes for gas, food, and lodging.

The old gas station, while not in operation, is adorned with authentic gas station signs from various companies and various eras. The Summit Inn's restaurant building is fairly plain by neon-era standards, but once entered, it's a roadologist's dream. Gasoline pumps from several companies are scattered around the dining area, with none of them being overly restored and still showing their authentic, realistic weathering. An authentic Route 66 highway marker sign hangs above the jukebox along with an array of old motor oil cans.

Veteran of the Summit Inn since 1960, Hilda Fish poses with owner C. A. Stevens, seen here with one of the many fortune-telling napkin dispensers that haunt the restaurant's tabletops. It's a chance to see in person one of the relics that *Twilight Zone* fans remember tormenting William Shatner in one classic episode. *"Hilda" calendars copyright Brown and Bigelow Inc. Photographed by permission*

Hilda Fish discovered the coincidentally named "Hilda" calendars in the early 1960s. She began signing them for the regulars, and it's been a Route 66 and Summit Inn tradition ever since. Retired truckers from all over the United States write every year for a "Hilda" calendar signed by Hilda Fish. *"Hilda" calendars copyright Brown and Bigelow Inc. Photographed by permission*

The Summit Inn's best attraction is not a thing but a person. Hilda Fish went to work at the restaurant in 1960 in her mid-30s. Her Germanic features and welcoming smile have been a favorite to truckers, cops, and other Summit Inn regulars ever since. Her name made for a coincidence resulting in one of today's most accessible Route 66 collectibles. Arizona artist Duane Bryers has a following among enthusiasts of Western art featuring the comfortingly familiar themes of cowboys and Indians shown working the trails, tracking game, and driving cattle. Bryers created a more cartoonish character named Hilda in 1956. With her crop of red hair, Ruebenesque plumpness, and innocent Mae West–style sexiness, the cartoon character named Hilda seemed an odd candidate for a pinup calendar, but a publisher gave her a shot in 1958, and she was a hit.

The Summit Inn discovered the coincidentally named "Hilda" calendars in the early 1960s, and Hilda Fish began signing them for truckers and travelers. The Summit Inn's Hilda Fish and Duane Bryers' "Hilda" calendar character thus cemented a mutual fan base. Retired truckers and travelers from around the world write to the Summit Inn every year for a "Hilda" calendar autographed by Hilda Fish.

The Summit Inn's current owner, C. A. Stevens, bought the landmark in 1966 and can tell of the many changes over the years that took the highway from one side of the restaurant to the other, the coming of the interstate era, and the changes in business climate that lead to his building the modern gas stations on the north side of the Summit Inn. He speaks with great pride about Hilda Fish's presence and the fun created by the "Hilda" calendar.

Proud of the Summit Inn's history, Stevens has created a line of fascinating postcards made from photos of an antique automobile meet at the Summit Inn in 1952. Antique cars collected in 1952 were "brass-era" cars from very early in the 1900s and up through roughly 1920. There were an abundance of them attending this long-ago meet. Mixed in with these brass-era cars are cars that were new in 1952 but that, today, hold the same fascination for collectors of old cars and Route 66 memorabilia. What was new then are today's classic cars, and what were old cars then are today's antiques.

Attached to the building and the artifacts thereof is the character of C. A. Stevens, and attached to the "Hilda" calendars and the restaurant is the character and memories of Hilda Fish.

"Oh, there was a terrible snowstorm in 1968 or '69," Hilda tells. "The snow was all the way up to the windowsills. We were open 24 hours a day back then, and I was on my fourth shift when I finally went home— almost 26 hours straight. The truckers were stuck here for three and four days. We had a lot of fires over the years

The Summit Inn's authentic shield, visible gas pump, and oil cans bring the remote Cajon Summit's driver-serving past alive for today's generations.

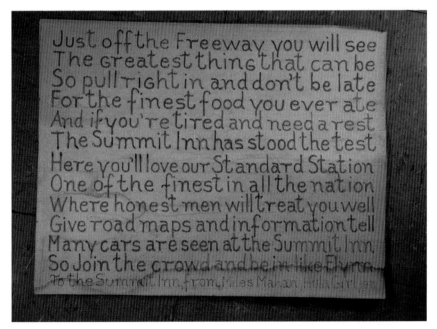

The late Miles Mehan was a 66 poet, collector, and general eccentric whose "Hulaville" stop between the Cajon Summit and Victorville, California, was a source of quizzical entertainment for travelers. In addition to Hulaville's bottle trees, windmills, and giant Hula dancer sign, Mehan posted many of his poems on signs and dedicated them to his local friends. This ode to the Summit Inn now resides in the Summit Inn collection.

"I have a mint-condition Coral Court matchbook now," Shellee Graham proudly tells, "but I found a tattered one the first time I was given a tour of the place from a little boy who, I think, was the son of the caretaker. It was so cool to get shown around by this nine-year-old boy and have a memento of it."

too. We had one burn clear up to the back of the building, and it was headed for the gas station. The wind was blowing something fierce, and C. A. actually burned his tie a little bit fighting the fire."

Memories like these and the tourists and truckers who lived them with her are what have made Hilda and the Summit Inn Route 66 legends.

SHELLEE GRAHAM— THE CORAL COURT'S KEEPER

In 1941, Watson Road was Route 66's path through St. Louis, Missouri's southwestern suburb Marlborough—just about the last piece of big city left in the rearview mirror of

Authentic Coral Court Motel artifacts and colors set the scene for Graham's bathroom.

a prewar westbound traveler. Ahead were smaller driver-serving towns like Cuba and Rolla with Springfield nearly a full day's drive in the distance. Between these bastions of civilization were miles of rural Missouri's fertile farms, woodsy greenery, and the Ozark Mountains' grades and curves.

Watson Road was the perfect location for a big motel to serve travelers beginning or ending a long, hard day's driving. The motel would catch a traveler's

eye with shining salmon and blue tiles, sweeping art deco lines, and crystalline glass brick—all in keeping with an incongruous underwater theme made stunning by its midwestern setting.

This motel was more than 20 years old in the early 1960s when a baby girl with big, brown eyes began toddling around Des Moines, Iowa.

Another 20 years took Route 66 and the motel past their primes and into the 1980s. The 1980s took the little girl into her prime with marriage and career taking her to suburban St. Louis.

Shellee Graham and the Coral Court Motel fell in love with each other in 1984, and ensuing years would see Graham photograph the whole and collect the fragments of the by-then decaying lodge with its growing no-tell-motel reputation. Little by little, Graham's collection has

Of the Coral Court items in Graham's bathroom, this bath towel seems to attract the most attention.

A glass block, bricks, bathroom tile, and other artifacts from the Coral Court Motel are proudly displayed in the Route 66 collection of Michael Wallis.

grown, making her one of the few specifically motel-oriented collectors along Route 66. Her art degree and career as a commercial artist gives Graham insights into the Coral Court's design and an appreciation toward its creators.

"I didn't choose the Coral Court; the Coral Court chose me," Graham laughs. "It was so perfect and beautiful. It was a masterpiece—an art deco gem. It was eight-and-a-half acres of art deco tile, shiny glazed brick, and rounded corners. When I first saw it in 1984, I was just amazed at how it survived, being that it was so wonderfully out of place. Its survival is part of what makes Route 66 fascinating. Anything from the '30s through the '60s fascinates me. There was nothing else like the Coral Court anywhere. The U-Drop Inn [in Shamrock, Texas] was beautiful, but it was one big piece. The Coral Court was dozens of scattered two-room units. The cars were hidden in the garages, and even though you were just feet from Watson Road, you were in this parklike setting that kind of let you get lost. It was like a minivacation. I met a couple who moved into the motel for five months while building their house, and they said they loved it for being peaceful and relaxing. Other people would go there for a weekend even though they lived in the St. Louis area just to get away from the stress of their lives."

The Coral Court Motel was demolished in the spring of 1995, but the lodge still inhabits the memories of local residents, past travelers, and Graham's collection, which includes bed linens, ashtrays, keys, postcards, tile, and glass bricks. Graham has created a Coral Court–themed bathroom in her home. Painted in the salmon and pink colors, the bathroom is adorned with a genuine Coral Court room number—46—on the wall along with enlarged photos of the motel and its famous sign. An ashtray holds a Coral Court matchbook that carries memories of Graham's discovery of the motel.

"I have a mint-condition Coral Court matchbook now, but I found a tattered one the

Fragments of the great Coral Court Motel have also found their way to the Michael Wallis collection.

A Coral Court postcard poses inside a genuine glass brick from the distinguished motel, and both pieces pose in the vast collection of Chicago area postcard expert Jeff Meyer. Artist and collector Jerry McClanahan says postcards touch him emotionally because they were always obtained at the famous locations they represent.

Neon extravaganza of the Munger Moss Motel in Lebanon, Missouri.

Genuine motel linen from the Jeff Meyer collection.

first time I was given a tour of the place from a little boy who, I think, was the son of the caretaker. It was so cool to get shown around by this nine-year-old boy and have a memento of it."

Graham's intense interest in the motel and its colorful history inspired her to write a book about it. *Tales From the Coral Court—Photos and Stories From a Lost Route 66 Landmark* covers the creation, personalities, and events that gave the motel an active personality beyond its static existence as an artistic, architectural, and historic piece. Included is the story of the Coral Court having been investigated by the FBI for having been the

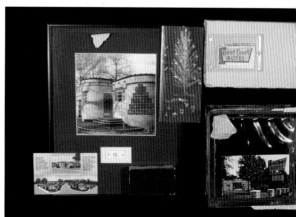

Steve Rider joins Shellee Graham as a collector of Coral Court memorabilia. These fragments live in Rider's Route 66 Garage in Albany, New York.
Marc Mirabile

hideout of kidnappers who murdered their victim even after the ransom had been paid. The suspects were apprehended at the Coral Court with half the ransom money, and Graham tells the story of the motel being searched by the FBI for the other half.

The book is illustrated with Graham's photographs, some of which have appeared in her touring photo show "Return to Route 66—Photographs from the Mother Road." Graham began gathering her photos in 1991 after she met a truck driver who had photographed much of Route 66. Her affection for the Coral Court, fascination with an era, commercial art profession, and memorabilia collection have dovetailed into a new direction that includes *Tales From the Coral Court*. Showing through it all is Graham's personality and sense of humor.

"The Coral Court is a field day for numerologists," says Graham. "Its address was 7755 Watson Road; it had 77 rooms; it was on Route 66, which was replaced by I-44. Who knows what cosmic forces gelled around that motel."

Don't forget all the Oldsmobile 88s that parked there, Shellee.

One of Route 66's most sought-after photo-ops— the restored Phillips 66 service station in McLean, Texas. It lives as a monument to the thousands who made their livings serving the driving public in the arena of gas, food, and lodging. Scott Piotrowski

CHAPTER 2

Getting There

Some people believe today's myths surrounding Route 66 will better serve the road's modern purpose than the realities of the past: painfully slow travel, treacherous curves and drops, and head-on collisions. Others feel that today's nostalgia forgets the realities too completely. While some of the road's realities are gravely unpleasant, others provide fascinating pictures of the past and the satisfaction of enjoying the "real thing."

"I hardly read fiction anymore. I read nonfiction because truth is stranger and far more interesting than fiction," says Dick Garrison, former president of the Old Town Victorville Property Owners Association, the founding organization of the California Route 66 Museum.

Garrison, whose father built his Ford dealership on Route 66's shoulder in Victorville in 1925, can see his sentiments reflected in the objects gathered by others whose focus lies on the realities of Route 66.

Sally Noe, Gallup, New Mexico's fiercely proud historian and booster, assembled her collection through the decades at the times the objects came into existence. She is an expert on the realities of Route 66's relationship and benefits to the Native Americans of the Southwest.

Jim Gilbert developed an affection for the steel and concrete of St. Louis, Missouri's Chain of Rocks Bridge and led an effort to provide Route 66 devotees with pieces of the bridge itself.

Retired postal worker Ken Turmel—a proud Oklahoman—sees a relationship between travel, the U.S. Postal Service, and Route 66, and has embarked on some astonishing works of art that teach as well as please.

The pride of suburban St. Louis—the Chain of Rocks Bridge—occupied the memories and captured the imagination of Jim Gilbert who lead the effort to preserve pieces of the bridge's decking and sold them to Route 66 enthusiasts to help fund a small portion of the bridge's restoration.

Jerry McClanahan of Texas and Jim Ross of Oklahoma find Route 66's greatest pleasures to be in the detective work of finding the road's old alignments, confirming their authenticity, and producing a line of maps to complement others' collections and help today's traveler find the real highway. Their love for the real thing is evident in their collections.

Route 66 was about travel. These enthusiasts find excitement in a piece of broken pavement, a vintage map that confirms an old alignment, a rusty oil can with an interesting alternative purpose, a postmark that teaches a lesson, or the products of an Indian craftsman whose living was improved by Route 66. For them, the best part of Route 66 is getting there.

SALLY NOE—
GALLUP, NEW MEXICO

Sally Noe gives walking tours of downtown Gallup, New Mexico. Once a town with a reputation for serious social and economic problems, Gallup has transformed into one of only three cities in the Land of Enchantment with a truly viable and economically successful downtown—a downtown so clean that Noe's walking tours include the clean, well-paved, well-lit alleys.

Born in 1926 in Kansas City, Missouri, Noe is brimming over with pride for Gallup where she's lived since being moved there at only three months of age when her father was sent to open the first J. C. Penney store in New Mexico. Noe's historical focus includes a strong reverence for Route 66 along with her detailed knowledge of Native American, wagon road, and railroad history. The Route 66 portion of Noe's collection revolves around the authentic experiences of tourists and business travelers who passed through Gallup in the Mother Road's heyday.

Mom, Dad, and the kids are represented in Noe's collection by the tourist items unique to Gallup—silver-and-turquoise jewelry for the lady of the family; leather

The famous giant arrows near Twin Arrows, Arizona.

Authenticity is key in Sally Noe's collection. The water bag is no nostalgic reproduction. It's the real thing as are the Conoco "Touraide" and the hand-painted tourist photo album, which exemplifies the crafted items made by the Navajo merchants of northwestern New Mexico.

Sally Noe, proud resident and historian of Gallup, New Mexico, stands with one of her prized Route 66 collectibles—a record of the song "Route 66" by Georgie Ald and His Orchestra.

Road life on Route 66 includes picking up souvenirs, such as maps and post cards like these in the jerry McClanahan collection.

bookmarks and playing card cases, painted ties, and silver cigarette lighters for the man of the house; and for the little ones, the Southwest's famous toy bows, arrows, Indian headdresses, and beaded dolls.

"One thing Gallup is noted for is that all its crafts are produced by Indians," Noe explains. "The clothing was bought from clothing companies, but all the paintings on them were painted by Indians. The Navajo rugs, pottery, and silver-and-turquoise jewelry were the first items to take off in popularity with travelers, but they were a bit expensive for the average tourist. The Gallup throw rug was developed to create a more affordable sale item. These rugs were about 30 inches by 30 inches. They sold for $2 to $5 as opposed to $10 for the large, hand-spun, hand-woven rugs."

According to Noe, an abundance of timber, rich coal deposits, and an all-weather route brought the A&P Railroad on its particular course through northwest New Mexico in the 1860s. Along with the easements, negotiations with Navajo, Hopi, and Zuni peoples included provisions for trading posts. Naturally, the all-weather route established by the railroads made Gallup part of Route 66's ideal path, and the benefits to the growing city were obvious to all.

"One of the old-timers told me he had hoped that if we got Route 66, each car would spend $10 in Gallup—for gas, food, campgrounds, and even souvenirs—and he was hoping for 50 cars a day. Our mayor in the 1920s, A. T. Hannett, was on the Good Roads committee along with Cyrus Avery. When they were talking about Route 66, he told the people of Gallup that they needed to campaign for the highway. It was the best route to California, and we needed to tell everyone about our attractions. The first thing Mr. Hannett did was pave seven blocks of Route 66 down Coal Avenue and [the street that would extend] Route 66. This was a way to say this was an up-and-coming community and not just a little farm town. Gallup was one meal stop away from any other town so every car coming through pretty much had to stop in Gallup."

In addition to being one meal stop away from the nearest small town with an eatery, Gallup was hours from any other town of any size, and as long as travelers were forced by that circumstance to spend the night in Gallup, they were inclined to soak up the atmosphere and gather the items that would be treasured by later Route 66 nostalgists.

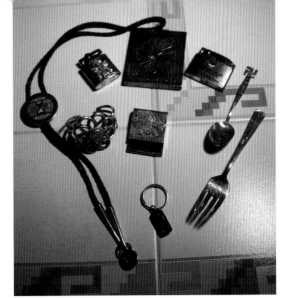

Route 66 was a boon to the Navajo crafters of the Southwest. Mom, Dad, and the kids are represented in the Noe collection by the tourist items unique to Gallup—silver-and-turquoise jewelry for the lady of the family; leather bookmarks and playing card cases, painted ties, and silver cigarette lighters for the man of the house; and for the little ones, the Southwest's famous toy bows, arrows, and Indian headdresses.

"Those cedar bows and arrows were all handmade," says Noe, a proud possessor of examples. "They were bought by the gross in this area. Every store that handled Indian merchandise had stacks of them because they couldn't keep them on the shelves. The headdresses were sold only because people thought Indians wore headdresses, which the Indians in this area did not. They were a very popular sale item—especially for a little boy; whereas, the colorful beaded dolls were very popular for little girls."

Hand-painted photo albums from the Indians and mass-produced travel guides through Gallup and New Mexico were popular among 66 travelers, and examples of both reside in Noe's collection. Many forget that one of the artists to perform the song "Route 66" was an orchestra leader named Georgie Ald, and a perfect copy of the record has found its way into Noe's appreciative hands.

Noe's contribution to the historical artifacts of Gallup can be seen at the Southwest Indian Foundation Cultural Center, a museum housed in Gallup's restored

A rare and special item in Noe's collection is the pearlescent "Radio Log" meant to be carried with travelers as a guide to radio stations all over the United States with plenty of space left for travelers to add stations as they discovered more. Dating to the early 1930s, the Radio Log can also aid enthusiasts of commercial radio history.

Santa Fe train station. Sally Noe and her daughter, Kathe, have produced a miniature representation of a typical New Mexico roadside town. Shaped roughly after the little, east-of-Gallup burg of Thoreau, the model captures the roadside grit of Route 66 through New Mexico complete with its dust, weathered buildings, and trash behind the fences. Those were the times Noe remembers well, and she included them all in her historically focused book *Greetings from Gallup—Six Decades of Route 66.* The book is filled with clear, detailed photos of Gallup dating from the late 1880s clear through Route 66's height as a highway, making for a great afternoon's read for the Route 66 devotee.

JIM GILBERT AND THE CHAIN OF ROCKS BRIDGE

"There are a lot of places I like to visit, and there are places I might like to live, but home is still home," Jim Gilbert says of his native St. Louis, Missouri. Born in 1943, Gilbert unwittingly witnessed Route 66's heyday and would later provide a pipeline to Mother Road enthusiasts stirred by tangible pieces of the highway's reality.

As the clock ticked past 1:45 P.M. on July 20, 1929, the Chain of Rocks Bridge opened and took travelers around St. Louis' congested downtown, making it one of Route 66's earliest bypasses of a big city. Today's St. Louis freeways are roughly arranged like a spoked wheel rimmed by two beltways. The Route 66 bypass of urban St. Louis formed what would later be called the Outer Belt by the locals and Interstate 270 by those looking at maps decades later. The bridge itself was an immense, dramatic, trestled structure reaching 5,400 feet across and high above the Mississippi River. It fit its surroundings with its meadow green paint and white concrete, and it passed two castle-shaped, brick-and-concrete water intakes in the river that feed the local water system.

It was and still is an impressive sight, but it had its problems. It was narrow and slick with a sudden bend in the middle that made for nervous confrontations between trucks traveling in opposite directions, and it's easy to imagine traffic jams forming at the toll plaza at the Missouri end as the traffic increased exponentially in post–World War II America.

The Chain of Rocks Bridge served its community and highway well; but times were changing, and the interstate era creeped toward this Jazz Age relic as it

Jim Gilbert with a fragment from Route 66's most famous bridge.

carried its burden into a fourth decade of operation. Just to its north, the concrete Interstate 270 bridge bypassed the Chain of Rocks' venerable girders in August 1966. The bridge remained open until approximately January 1970. During this coexistence between old and new, the tollbooth disappeared, traffic quieted, and it became a bridge to nowhere. Its days were numbered.

"As long as I can remember, the Chain of Rocks Bridge was there, and of course, I remember crossing it all the time when it was open," Gilbert recalls. "I really wasn't that aware of its closing. It wasn't really a big day when the bridge was closed because the other bridge had been opened for a few years. I don't remember any big headlines. It just quietly died. After a few years, I began to wonder when I was going to be driving to work and see the explosions as the Corps of Engineers blew it up."

As the decades unfolded into the 1970s, 1980s, and 1990s, Gilbert began to slowly treasure his childhood and young adult memories of the Chain of Rocks Bridge and trips to California on the train tracks that followed Route 66. Upon hearing in the mid-1990s that

The Chain of Rocks Bridge looking doomed in 1994.

an effort was underway by public and private concerns to open a park with the bridge connecting its two halves, Gilbert immediately became involved. Phase by phase, Gilbert was abreast of the bridge's restoration process. When the time came to repair the decking, Gilbert flashed on an idea that would provide the world with some of its most authentic collectable pieces of Route 66's reality.

"In the planning of the construction phase, I realized the decking of the bridge was actually in better shape than the McKinley Bridge, which is still in use in downtown St. Louis," Gilbert says. "I had heard in September of 1997 that they were going to start breaking up some of [the] weak portions of the decking. They had chalked off some of the areas they were going to jackhammer out. Most of these sections were pretty small, but there were a lot of them. There were no vast sections that were going to be done all at once. I was at home cutting my grass one morning when it hit me out of the blue. I asked myself what they were going to do with all that old decking. I called the lady who was in charge of managing some of the operation. I told her we should try and save some of the decking that Route 66 enthusiasts would kill to get. The money raised by selling the pieces really wouldn't put a dent in the millions of dollars spent refurbishing the bridge, of course, but it was still worth doing, I thought. I called one of the construction guys, and he agreed to dump a truckload of it in my yard. My wife didn't know about it, of course, but when she saw it later that day, she just shook her head because she knew I was up to something with the bridge. Most of the pile was just plain old concrete that

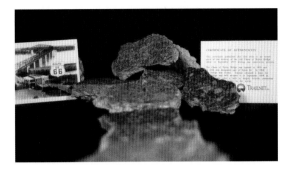

you couldn't tell anything from, but others were pieces of identifiable decking coated with rust from the bridge. Most of the pieces were about 4 inches square."

These 4-inch pieces vibrate with the Chain of Rocks Bridge's status as a distinguished survivor in the interstate era. A piece of this bridge speaks of the legions of workers and vacationers who had the opportunity to use this steel-and-concrete masterpiece.

KEN TURMEL—POSTMASTER OF AMERICA'S MAIN STREET

Route 66's often-mentioned heyday was in full swing when Ken Turmel was born in Los Angeles, California, in the mid-1950s. His family roots stretched far to the east, and these roots led to one of Ken's toughest accomplishments—gathering every postmark along America's Main Street. It's a simple enough sounding idea, but efforts to make it interesting took Turmel to bypassed towns, state capitals, famous signers, and into searches for just the right special occasion postmarks.

The cornerstones for the project were set in Turmel's childhood.

"My parents moved to California from New Hampshire in the early 1950s," Turmel remembers. "They would get homesick every summer, and starting about 1957, they would make their yearly summer vacation back home to see Mom and Dad in Manchester, New Hampshire, on old Route 66. This is pre-interstate, and Route 66 was the main way to get most of the way to New Hampshire from California."

The images of Route 66's roadside were stamped into Turmel's child's-eye view of America as he watched them go by, but it would be years before he realized the full impression the highway had made on him. The images were filed away in Turmel's mind as he grew up, did a

Pieces of the Chain of Rocks Bridge with certificates of authenticity. "In the planning of the construction phase, I realized the decking of the bridge was actually in better shape than the McKinley Bridge, which is still in use in downtown St. Louis," Jim Gilbert tells. "I had heard in September of '97 that they were going to start breaking up some of [the] weak portions of the decking. They had chalked off some of the areas they were going to jackhammer out. Most of these sections were pretty small, but there were a lot of them. I was at home cutting my grass one morning when it hit me out of the blue. I asked myself what they were going to do with all that old decking. I called the lady who was in charge of managing some of the operation. I told her we should try and save some of the decking that Route 66 enthusiasts would kill to get. The money raised by selling the pieces really wouldn't put a dent in the millions of dollars spent refurbishing the bridge, of course, but it was still worth doing, I thought. I called one of the construction guys, and he agreed to dump a truckload of it in my yard."

Originally from California, Ken Turmel has proudly adopted suburban Oklahoma City as his hometown. Retired from the U.S. Postal Service, Turmel has employed his intimate knowledge of the postal system to create works of art by gathering commemorative postmarks on maps of his own design. His first work, the "Adventure Centennial Document," celebrated Oklahoma's famous Cherokee Strip land run of the 1890s. Its success lead to Turmel's creation of "Oklahoma and Friends," a map depicting Oklahoma and its seven surrounding states with historical references illustrated by the postmarks. The two lead to Turmel's crack at Route 66.

stint in the military in the 1970s, moved to Oklahoma, and worked 16 years for the United States Postal Service.

In 1993, Turmel combined his deep knowledge of the postal system with his artistic leanings and affection for his adopted Oklahoma. He created a map of the pan-shaped state and began gathering dozens of postmarks from the communities affected by northwestern Oklahoma's massive Cherokee Strip land run of the 1890s. Titled the "Adventure Centennial Document," this commemoration of Sooner State history got the piece displayed at Oklahoma's famous 101 Ranch where it caught the eye of author Michael Wallis who encouraged Turmel to toil toward a similar opus on Route 66. It began in 1994.

Two years and 28,661 miles later—more than the circumference of the Earth—Turmel's undertaking was completed and dubbed *Sixty-six and More. . . .*

The "Sixty-six" half of the work's title refers to Turmel having gathered a postmark from every post office along 66, including one from the Cadiz, California, office on its last day in operation and a mark from the Lamont, Illinois, office shortly before losing its name and postmark to absorption into the neighboring Bolingbrook location. The "and More . . ." half alludes to the state capitals, famous people, limited-edition postage stamps, and special commemorative postmarks that are used only for 30 days before being destroyed permanently at the end of the commemorative period.

Famous people include media favorites such as "Route 66" songwriter Bobby Troup, *Route 66* TV series star Martin Milner, and Jim Rogers—son of the late, great humorist Will Rogers. Ron Shutiva, governor of New Mexico's Acoma Tribe has his signature on Turmel's map along with Lucille Hammons, longtime gas station owner in Hydro, Oklahoma, author Michael Wallis, and retired Missouri State Trooper Ira Letterman.

When the postal service issues a new stamp, it appears in only a single city for the first day before being released to the entire United States the following day. Called a "first-day issue," these stamps are meaningful to stamp collectors, and "Sixty-six and More . . ." has four representing Santa Fe, Amarillo for Cal Farley's Boy's Town, Oklahoma City for the Indian Dance stamp by artist Keith Birdsong, and St. Louis for the Blue Bird Stamp. In recognition of the Texas Fun Run, every town in the Panhandle had a special postmark for Route 66, and all are found on the map.

Sixty-six and More . . . comes with a booklet of facts, thoughts, trivia, and quiz questions. Coming through the work are the personality of Ken Turmel and the adventures he had while traveling the road to gather all that information. Supai, Arizona, at the bottom of Havasu Canyon, a side branch of the Grand Canyon, is the only place in the United States where the mail is still delivered by horse because of the narrow, winding footpath that is this Native American community's only road. Turmel transported his original map by burro 10 miles down into the canyon for Supai's postmark.

"It was a very humbling experience because [the Supai] don't have TVs, aren't into radio. . . . The waves for TV and radio don't even go down into the Grand

Ken Turmel's Mother Road masterpiece, "Route 66 and More . . ." Turmel logged more than 28,000 miles to create this one work.

Canyon. Everything that's down in the canyon—every can of Coca-Cola, every hamburger patty, every last sheet of toilet paper—is hand-carried down in there by those Indians. It's an amazing place."

Turmel was well into the project when the images of traveling 66 in his childhood finally came flooding back from dormancy.

"[The importance of Route 66] really didn't click with me until I was working on this project in 1995," he says. "I was driving the old route to get these postmarks, and I started recognizing some of the places I had been as a kid. For example, I was at the Colorado River, and there was a little dock where you could go swimming. Whenever we would pass through there, it was really early in the morning, and I would always say, 'Hey Dad, let's stop, let's stop,' and my dad would say, 'No, we gotta get there, we gotta get there.' When I was working on this project, I took the time to go down to the Colorado River to swim and do some relaxing, and it was right then that it hit me and made the connection between the man and the boy in me. This was someplace I wanted to go when I was a little boy, and I didn't have a chance to do it until I was a grown man. Then, I started seeing things in a little different light as I was traveling doing this Route 66 project. A lot of boyhood memories came to me that were completely forgotten, and they were revamped by making this trip. Right then at the Colorado River, I realized this was an important facet of my life."

JERRY MCCLANAHAN— TEXAS ARTIST

The 1950s saw Jerry McClanahan's father do what many Oklahomans had done in the 1930s—move to California seeking work in the oil fields. The year was 1959, and the family's new home was Castaic, California, along the Golden State's famous and historic Ridge Route.

McClanahan was a small child when the family began making regular trips east on Route 66 to visit family in Arkansas, and these trips implanted the images that would form McClanahan's passion for Route 66 and the basis for his artistic education, career, and pastime.

"The 1960s were the time when the interstates were just starting to replace Route 66," McClanahan recalls. "Every year there would be another town bypassed. I

Artist Jerry McClanahan with two of his paintings made famous by their appearance of his popular line of postcards.

remember when they bypassed Albuquerque in the mid-'60s, my mom and I talked about it, and we really missed seeing what was going on in downtown Albuquerque. As the 1960s progressed, I wasn't looking forward to the trips as much because I missed going through all the small towns where you'd see Indians, cool signs, shop windows, and people walking around. Of course, my dad loved it because he would drive straight through. My dad believed that on a vacation, you should get to your destination as quickly as you could.

"We hit Route 66 in Victorville, California, and we made it all the way to Fort Smith, Arkansas, in about 30 hours. Now, I'm the opposite because I believe the travel is as important a part of the trip as getting there. I would be in the back seat of the car seeing all this neat stuff go by in a blur, and I guess it kind of set me up for what I'm doing now. I couldn't wait to get back out there and see all the things I missed."

Passing and missing roadside scenes and culture were temporary for McClanahan.

"We took a trip on Route 66 in 1981, and I kind of took my revenge. I made my father stop at everything," he says. "We stopped at Meteor Crater, Clines Corners, all the trading posts—everything. The interstates are great if you're trying to get somewhere in a hurry, but if I have any time at all I want to get on the old concrete road and hear it go ka-thump, ka-thump, ka-thump. . . . I could see I was missing a lot on that 1981 trip. I could see there were old roads running off around the roads we were on, but I couldn't tell if any

Jerry McClanahan's collection centers around the realities of actual travel. Having been exploring Route 66 since 1981, McClanahan is most concerned with getting there. His collection of authentic maps has helped McClanahan and Jim Ross confirm old alignments of the highway and create their line of travel maps to the remnants of Route 66 for the modern traveler.

of them had at times been Route 66 or not. I started collecting old maps, and what not, so I could drive as much of the old pavement as I could and photograph all the old gas stations and things."

McClanahan's collection is an information bank with maps being a focal object. Accurate and to scale, old maps were McClanahan's tools for finding the old road while postcards provided photographic accuracy and archeological information for roadside artifacts.

While working toward his bachelor of fine arts degree at the University of North Texas, McClanahan became frustrated with an art world where the "unusual" had become "average." Impressionistic painting ruled the art scene, making reality-bending a run-of-the-mill norm. McClanahan found reality itself to be a much more interesting art subject, and he perfected capturing the aluminum surfaces of jet aircraft and the chrome and waxed surfaces of old American cars.

As the 1980s progressed, Route 66 languished unnoticed by most with only a handful of dedicated outlanders like McClanahan paying any attention, but as a few books caught the public imagination in the late 1980s, the stage was set for the Mother Road revival of the 1990s, and McClanahan's love for the road, artistic training, and information–gold mine collection dovetailed into a successful, vindicated career.

Through a letter to a travel magazine in the early 1990s, McClanahan found Jim Ross of Arcadia, Oklahoma, was also researching the previous paths of Route 66. The two joined forces, with Ross specializing in the eastern half of 66 and McClanahan focusing on the west. Through Ross' company, Ghost Town Press, the team produced an eight-map set that takes the enthusiast through each state on Route 66. McClanahan's artistry

illustrates and entertains, and information from both men informs and guides. The map set was a hit.

The successes continued as McClanahan produced a set of postcards featuring his oil paintings which contain McClanahan's two passions—cars and the Route 66 roadside. While mythical and somewhat whimsical, the paintings also capture the reality of Route 66. The cars are accurate, and the roadside scenes are presented as they really were, with McClanahan's paintbrush having restored them to their former glory.

From the beginning, McClanahan's attitude toward preserving the reality of Route 66 has led to a well thought out ethical philosophy toward collecting the artifacts found laying at the roadside. This is illustrated by a special sign in McClanahan's collection—a silhouette of Arizona's famous Jack Rabbit and the words *381 miles*.

"I want things left where they are, but I'm afraid of what will happen [to the pieces that are in immediate danger]," McClanahan says. "I bought the Jack Rabbit sign from the caretaker of the Frontier Bar and Museum near Santa Rosa. It was tied to the fence because someone had found it years before lying in a field. It wasn't in the original place, and I wasn't hurting any historical record by obtaining it. I didn't swipe it. I paid for it. I have a big sign that simply says 'Snakes' in big letters that I found lying in a ditch weathering and rotting. I asked the owner of a roadside business if I could take it. I'm all for rescuing things, but it's always best to get permission. If

Between McClanahan's familiarity with the western half of 66 and Jim Ross' knowledge of the eastern half, the team put together the eight-map set with the goal of connecting the remaining portions of Route 66 as much as possible and giving a history lesson with the text along the way.

"I want things left where they are, but I'm afraid of what will happen [to the pieces that are in immediate danger]," says Jerry McClanahan. "I bought the Jack Rabbit sign from the caretaker of the Frontier Bar and Museum near Santa Rosa, New Mexico. It was tied to the fence because someone had found it years before lying in a field. It wasn't in the original place, and I wasn't hurting any historical record by obtaining it. I didn't swipe it. I paid for it. I have a big sign that simply says 'Snakes' in big letters that I found laying in a ditch weathering and rotting. I asked the owner of a roadside business if I could take it. I'm all for rescuing things, but it's always best to get permission. If it's still in its original place and not in any immediate danger, leave it up so someone else can come along and take a picture of it."

Authentic signs that got people there in the Jim Ross collection. *Scott Piotrowski*

it's still in its original place and not in any immediate danger, leave it up so someone else can come along and take a picture of it. There can be a lot of argument about it, and I guess it's kind of a case-by-case basis."

JIM ROSS—
ARCADIA, OKLAHOMA

Jim Ross' prized possession is his authentic Route 66 highway marker from the 1920s, as one might imagine; but high on his list are much more surprising and "humble" artifacts.

"I have three flattened oil cans that were part of the roofing shingles on the awning of the Humble Oil Company gas station between San Jon and Tucumcari, New Mexico, on the old alignment of 66," Ross happily tells. "These cans are weathered and rusty, but they serve as a direct connection to that whole era of travel—the days when the guy came out and checked your oil and opened the oil cans with a can opener. Evidently, this Humble station saved hundreds of used oil cans and

The hard facts of Route 66's many paths are the focus of Jim Ross' interest in the highway, and markers such as this denoted the Mother Road's right-of-way. Scott Piotrowski

The concrete history of Route 66 can be determined by historians and collectors such as Jim Ross who can date and confirm the various alignments of the highway through examination of its fragments. Scott Piotrowski

used them for roofing shingles. It's important because it's an integral part of our history as Americans because of the vivid experiences of the Dust Bowl, the Depression, and the post–World War II tourist boom that really made the highway legendary. These oil cans were part of those experiences."

Ross epitomizes the self-styled Route 66 collector who sees meaning in the forgotten debris forsaken next to the two-lane artery as the interstate era dawned. The individual items may not have monetary value, but they have deep significance to those who know the road's story or are looking for fragments of another time and the actual tools of getting there, whether elegant roadside markers or splintered fragments that only become fascinating when the accompanying explanation is related.

Ross was born in Florida in 1949, but the Oklahoma City area has been his home since the late 1950s.

"When the TV show ran, I was in that 10 to 14 age group and, of course, idolized Todd and Buzz, and there was a lot of inspiration, fantasy, and wishful thinking there," Ross says. "I really didn't have any connection with Route 66 from my midadolescence until I was in my late 30s. Around 1989, when Wallis' book was published, there was an article about Route 66 in the local paper, and as I read it, it just hit me that I really wanted to go see this road. I was especially interested to do it because it was in my own backyard."

Ross had discovered Tom Snyder's *Route 66 Traveler's Guide* and a brochure by the Oklahoma tourism department covering Route 66, but Ross wanted more detail on his home state and began a quest for detail that lead to his publishing his own guidebook to Route 66 in Oklahoma in 1992. Through a letter to the *Mother Road Journal*, Ross met Jerry McClanahan—one of the pioneering roadologists who had been traveling, collecting, and photographing Route 66 since the early 1980s. With Ross' strength of knowledge lying in the eastern half of America's Main Street and McClanahan's strength lying in the western half, the two combined their knowledge and McClanahan's artistic skill to produce their popular eight-map set to Route 66.

As this collaboration was producing a valuable guide to Route 66 travelers, Ross began to assemble his own collection of Mother Road memorabilia. His collection soon had a star piece.

"My most prized possession is an authentic Route 66 highway shield," he says. "It's exceptionally rare because it's still on the pole it was mounted on. It doesn't have any paint left on it and it's pitted with rust, but it's the real thing. I have reason to believe it's one of the inaugural signs that was put up in 1926 because it shared its pole with a smaller shield with an *R* on it denoting that the highway was going to make a right turn. Under both of those is a sign showing 66 was sharing its pavement with Oklahoma Highway 7, which came into existence in 1924. When 66 was born in 1926, it followed the path of Oklahoma 7. Sixty-six and 7 were only combined for four years from 1926 to 1930. You know it's authentic because it's still mounted to the pole and all the bolts are corroded in place. I bought it from a country boy up in Davenport, Oklahoma, who found it on his property. He knew it was probably worth something. I didn't get a bargain, but he was willing to sell it."

Here are two styles of authentic road markers. The shields faded in and out of style in different places at different times, making the exact dates of the changes in style the subject of intense debate. Whether an inaugural shield from the 1920s or one of the last to grace the highway in the 1980s, a shield is a prized and meaningful possession for the Main Street devotee.

The Automobile Club of Southern California marked the highways of the Mojave Desert with these porcelain-coated signs. The National Old Trails Highway would later become Route 66, and this sign marked the way between Barstow and Victorville, California, and dates to approximately 1914.

As with the oil can shingle, Ross' collection boasts smaller, quieter pieces that still hold much meaning to Ross. These include a piece of stucco from the Painted Desert Trading Post found crumbling in the eastern Arizona sand, a pocket-sized fragment of concrete decking from the Chain of Rocks Bridge, and a sign advertising Texas' Regal Reptile Ranch with the words *Snakes, Alligators, Gila Monsters.*

"I'm very careful not to take anything that should be left there," Ross adds. "A person could argue you shouldn't take anything at all, but when you have a situation like the Painted Desert Trading Post where you have pieces of the decaying stucco lying on the ground

Nothing was more important to "getting there" than the pavement itself, and even pocket-sized fragments give enthusiasts the gritty, weathered feel of history. The two round concrete pieces shown here were discovered in the mid-1990s when road construction crews working in the Fontana, California, area performed core samples for improvements. They are reputed to date to 1929. The large piece is from the steepest of the Mother Road's original alignment up California's Cajon Pass, and it's made of the original circa-1920 concrete with a later repaving of asphalt over the top.

Bill Shea, the venerable Springfield, Illinois, gasoline man, shows the world a piece of Route 66's 1920s brick alignment through the central portion of the Land of Lincoln.

that [are] just going to be lost in the sand anyway, it can be an opportunity to save something that may soon be lost to the elements. If you're not taking a hammer and chisel to get something loose, it's probably okay."

Oklahoma City's Route 66 neighbor to the east is a pleasant little time machine of a town known as Arcadia—home to the restored and much photographed Round Barn. A short drive farther east, the experienced Route 66 seeker will quickly recognize an old alignment splitting from the main road and disappearing into the woods. Ross makes his home on this old alignment where he has effectively come to collect the road itself.

"The road where I live is a 1-mile loop around a low hill that was bypassed in 1952 in favor of an improved alignment around the other side of the hill," he says. "It ties in to the newer road on both ends. This road is in original, unaltered, near pristine condition and consists of two different surfacing types, which abut near the mid-point. One type is pure Portland concrete. The other is a concrete base covered with 2 inches of rock asphalt and with 9-inch concrete strips along each edge. They are

Bob Waldmire is a founding member of the Historic Route 66 Association of Illinois, Cozy Dog heir, and former owner of the Old Route 66 Visitors Center in Hackberry, Arizona. He combines all these traits with his artistic abilities to create some of Route 66's most informative modern collectibles.

Collector Jeff Meyer is seen here traveling with an authentic *Guidebook to Highway 66* by Jack Rittenhouse from 1946. Rittenhouse had traveled Route 66 in the early days after World War II and created this detailed little book filled with directions, scenic advice, and historical references. Accurate reprints of this book proved extremely popular through the nostalgia movement of the 1990s.

known respectively as a Bates and a Modified Bates–type roadway. In the spring of 1999, I prepared a National Register nomination packet, which was submitted in the fall and accepted onto the register on November 30. The property's historical significance comes from the engineering aspects of the roadway and its value as a surviving example of road construction of the era, which, of course, is part of our transportation history."

Ross' collection contains things as grand as the road and its markers and things as small as a decades-old, rusted-out gasoline can which occupies a small shelf in his kitchen along with pieces of brick and electric pole insulators.

"Some people see this stuff and think I'm crazy. We just have to realize that it's beyond some people's imagination."

More than mere postcards and maps, Waldmire's products are mini-history books filled with the histories, cultures, and textures of the highway's many regions.

CHAPTER 3

Working The Route

They never think they're very interesting. It can take a journalist or historian some time to convince an average-seeming person to recount the events of his or her life. Many of the interview subjects come right out and say, "I don't know why you want to talk with me. I'm not very interesting. I'm just a cop, truck driver, car dealer, or gas station attendant. Why would anyone want to know about me?"

Having said this, he or she will eventually be persuaded by the historian to sit for an interview, and this uninteresting, average, older person will begin recounting the events of his or her working life—the common occurrences of what, to him or her, were just the daily grind of making a living over the years. Along the way, they describe things they don't think are important like the make and model of a car, the buzzing sound of a neon sign, reaching for a gearshift of a big truck, what it's like to be shot by a criminal, driving 100 miles per hour on a curving road, or just how curvy and dangerous a road was. Only a person who was there can describe these things and give younger people insights into past circumstances impossible to experience today. They will describe their friends and enemies, their loves and hates, their wins and losses. . . . After a while, they will laugh and cry easily, taking the listeners on the intellectual and emotional roller coaster their life was made of.

Route 66 enthusiasts love John Steinbeck for this touching, frightening account of the Joad family's flight from the Dust Bowl in the *Grapes of Wrath*. Steinbeck was one of the masters at illustrating that an average life is as rich, full, and fascinating as the life of any

"My neon was done by Inland Neon," Pat Matlach explains. "Mike Weimer is the one whose signature is on the picture [from which the plans for the neon were made]. I had two of these big signs down at the other place, and Mike Weimer had done those. When I moved here, we took one of those signs, moved it here, and added the arrow. It was a [walking flash] arrow at that time when the city incorporated and passed some sign ordinances, I had to stop the flashing."

Missouri State Highway
Patrol Safety Squadron,
circa 1940. Tom Pasley,
front row at right.
*Missouri State Highway
Patrol collection*

from the same location fronting America's Main Street
for nearly five decades.

Don Shuey didn't think he was very interesting, but
he drove a loaded produce truck twice a week through the
Mojave Desert's 115-degree heat on 24-hour roundtrips.

Did Bill Pierce think he was interesting? Not really—
until he started telling the tale of having his truck roll
away from him—driverless—down Route 66.

Their accounts serve as examples of the fascinating
average lives lead on Route 66.

SERGEANT CHESTER HENRY—
ILLINOIS STATE POLICE

There wasn't a lot of pavement to be found in rural
Illinois in the early days of highway travel, and to the
residents of the state, Route 66's smooth pavement was
called the hard road.

"Route 66 got so successful that it put itself out of
business because it got so busy and dangerous," says
Sergeant Henry. "That's why the five interstates were built
to replace it. Sixty-six was built along old cattle trails, and
down in Missouri, there were a lot of real narrow bridges
that weren't necessarily engineered for safety at that time.
But, a lot of good things happened out there too. People
went west to a better life during the Dust Bowl. People
used it to go on vacation. People used it to make a good
living with all the service stations, restaurants, and motels
that sprung up along the highway."

In the world of Route 66, Henry is a relatively recent
addition, joining the Illinois State Police in 1957. His
patrol district was very large, covering Route 66 from
Dwight to McLean roughly 75 miles to the south. This
encompassed five counties, the midsized, connected
cities of Bloomington and Normal, and other highways
on either side of 66 for quite a distance.

Henry's motivations for having been a policeman
seem social. He just likes people.

"Just the idea I was out there to help people [was my
favorite part of my job]," he says. "I'd get to talk with
people while rendering assistance or meeting them in
restaurants. I got to know people in all the little towns
from Dwight to McLean—the service people, the mechanics at the garages, the judges, and even the funeral home
people. I got to know everybody and have some very
pleasant memories of them. I even enjoyed talking with
the people I stopped and finding out where they were

famous celebrity or captain of industry—that average
people are brimming with knowledge and passion.

Route 66 was a passionate, eventful place, and as
with any other ongoing flurry, the people who experienced it firsthand can relate information that can be
found nowhere else. As the twenty-first century begins,
America is losing the Route 66 generation, and their
memories need to be preserved so Americans years—
possibly hundreds of years—into the future can experience Route 66 from that precious firsthand standpoint.

Buzz Banks didn't think he was very interesting,
but this retired highway cop and author escorted tanks
on Route 66 through the Mojave Desert with General
Patton during World War II.

Gene Tinnin didn't think he was very interesting,
but this Missouri cop was shot four times on the shoulder of Route 66.

Tom Pasley didn't think he was very interesting, but
he designed the popular logo of a large police department that has been in constant use on Route 66 and
other highways for more than a half-century.

Chester Henry, a "hard road cop," didn't think he
was very interesting until he was asked to lecture Route
66 devotees about keeping the road safe during violent
snowstorms and keeping himself safe through a couple
of attempts on his life.

Pat Matlach didn't think he was very interesting,
but Route 66 was about cars, and he has sold them

from. I enjoyed helping people when they were broke down and getting them shelter when it was cold."

Henry's favorite roadside establishments, like the Dixie Truckers Home in McLean or the N&J Cafe south of Dwight, were often good for tipping off the state police about drunken drivers or suspicious characters, and Henry chased them down. An escaped convict had taken a car for a test drive at a dealership in Michigan and made it his getaway car, but he made the mistake of taking the car into the jurisdiction of the Illinois State Police.

"A trooper caught [the convict] near Odell," Henry remembers. "Once he stopped the car, he [the convict] grabbed a bottle of whiskey and a 12-gauge shotgun and ran off into a cornfield. Now, a bottle of whiskey and a loaded shotgun is as dangerous a combination as you can get. We had to get the police dogs, and three of us troopers had to go [into a field of tall corn] to catch him. We finally did catch him when one of the police dogs got him down on the ground, and we cuffed him."

It sounds like a safe enough arrest, but for the officers the rest of the story represents a narrow escape from death. Henry and a sergeant were standing behind a police car to avoid being shot. The desperado admitted later that he started shaking a fence trying to lure the officers out so he could shoot them and take their police car.

"We came so close to getting shot on that one that the sergeant, who was eligible for retirement, retired!"

While the public at large wasn't always all that concerned about drunken driving until the 1980s, policemen have always known the realities of the intoxicated driver. The GM&O Railroad runs through Bloomington, and Route 66 crossed the tracks atop a large overpass.

"There was a drunk going north in the southbound lanes, and you can't see over that overpass," Henry explains. "I saw him, got ahead of him, and got the traffic stopped. There was a divider, and I couldn't get over to the other side so I jumped out of my squad car with the red lights going, and I flagged the traffic to a stop. I barely had enough time to flag to a stop some big rigs

that were running side by side. If I hadn't stopped those trucks, that man would have been dead, but I don't think he thanked me for saving his life because he went to jail."

Proximity of the monumental metropolis of Chicago to Henry's rural patrol district combined with the icy nature of the Midwest made north-central Illinois a dangerous place to the travelers, truckers, and cops of the hard road. One Easter Sunday in the early 1960s, a truck turned over in a blinding snowstorm between Lexington and Towanda.

"Once the first guy hit that truck, everyone came up behind him, and before they could get traction to stop, there were 17 vehicles involved in the wreck. We had to get several ambulances to deal with all the injuries. We never really did determine who hit whom. One fellow said, 'I was in my car, and I got hit three times. I don't know who hit me.' Now, on some of these big toll roads and expressways up in Chicago, these kinds of wrecks were commonplace, but we weren't used to that down in our area."

Some intersections were far more dangerous than others.

Sergeant Chester Henry kept motorists safe through the icy winters of rural Illinois. Donning his slick uniform, he recounts his stories as a guest speaker at various Route 66 functions.

You can't keep a good man down. Captain Gene Tinnin of the Missouri State Highway Patrol revisits the very spot where he was shot four times in 1956. It's on Route 66, just near the Gasconade River.

ble than anyone else. I think their appearance was their downfall."

Sergeant Henry is one of the few police officers to participate in the modern resurgence of interest in the Mother Road that blossomed in the 1990s and progressed into the twenty-first century. He gives the kinds of public talks to Route 66 enthusiasts that can be heard only from those who were there. He believes younger people are interested in Route 66 and his stories because the stories they hear from their parents and grandparents make them hunger for more.

"Sixty-six is probably the last frontier," he says. "The interstates are kind of impersonal. There are no traffic lights, and you have to pull off the interstates to get any services, and it's just not the same. It's kind of a romantic thing. [The young people are shown all the roadside America that once was], and the young people say, 'Hey, we don't have those things anymore, and there's not going to be another Route 66.' They want to go back and see how it was."

"The intersection of U.S. 24 and 66 in Chenoa was particularly bad," Henry says. "It was engineered just like all the other intersections, but it had a lot of bad wrecks. Sixty-six southbound came around a curve approaching the intersection as did the northbound lanes because 66 bows out around the town of Chenoa. It wasn't straight-on, and that was probably the problem. Dwight and Odell had a lot of accidents too. I think the reason Dwight had so many accidents was because it had the first traffic light out of Chicago at that time. People weren't expecting it to be there. With all the intersections, Route 66 was really a fairly dangerous highway. There were a lot of accidents. When the traffic went onto I-55 later, and all those traffic-signal intersections were bypassed, then the traffic danger went down a lot."

The changing times of the late 1960s weren't always comfortable for a policeman, but Henry remembers the era that ended Route 66 with the good-natured humor of a classic midwesterner when he tells the story of a car with a couple in it who seemed more interested in smooching than driving.

"I thought the girl was driving with a male passenger, but when I got them stopped and checked them out, the driver was a long-haired boy! His hair was a lot longer than the girl's. [Hippies] were no more trou-

CAPTAIN GENE TINNIN— MISSOURI STATE HIGHWAY PATROL

Why would a man shot four times on Route 66 remember one inch of that road fondly? One answer could be a grit that may be lost in America today—the kind of grit that makes a man parachute into the Battle of the Bulge during World War II and face thousands of Germans with guns. Gene Tinnin needed this grit again at age 27 when he joined the Missouri State Highway Patrol in 1949 and experienced many bad days on Route 66 between Conway and Waynesville. There were days when ice slid cars into ditches by the hundreds and made a cop work 24-hour shifts, when holiday weekends were marred by the traffic deaths of children, and when a cop had to deal with a drunken driver who wanted a fight.

But, there were good days, too, as when Tinnin moved the family of a soldier injured in a crash into his home for two weeks while the soldier recovered in the hospital—thus cementing a 25-year friendship.

Tinnin's voice bestows down-home Ozark charm as he tells stories from his 32-year career: Lebanon, Missouri, is "Leb'nin," and Route 66 is "Rhaaaht Sixtah-Six." However pleasant to the good citizens of central Missouri, Tinnin's charm was unwelcome to midwestern evildoers,

and while many ran away, none ever got away. Tinnin caught every maggot he chased down Route 66 but modestly attributes his success to a lot of luck, road-clogging highway traffic, the Ozarks' hilly terrain, and expert marksmanship that convinced even the most hardened criminal to pull over when the rear window of his car exploded.

Tinnin didn't win every confrontation, though. September 19, 1956, was Tinnin's "most troubling day." It was a hot, dry day on a hilltop near the Gasconade River 13 miles east of Lebanon.

"I was driving along on 66 there in my patrol car, and I came over this hill, and there was this Chevrolet car facing me in my lane. I turned around and stopped him to check him out a little bit and also warn him about being too anxious and doing something as careless as trying to pass on a curve near a hill like that," Captain Tinnin recalls. "Well, that particular day, I wasn't feeling too aggressive because I was having a painful back problem, and I didn't follow him to his car door when I asked him to get his driver's license and papers on the car. He came back to me with a .32 Colt revolver and fired four times. [The first two shots] struck me in the knee and side, and that one in my

side lodged near my spine. As I fell back, he fired two more times, and the first of those two went through my neck—in and out—missing my spinal cord by a centimeter or so. The last shot hit the ammunition pouch on my belt and lodged there. That put me in the hospital for 16 days, and it was 60 days before I was back at work.

"He was charged with stealing the car, and he had killed his cousin in Chicago and was running to the West Coast when I had my encounter with him. He was later tried for assault with a deadly weapon with intent to kill, and he was sentenced to 25 years."

Most of the time, it worked the other way with the criminals going to jail and Tinnin going home safe with a great story to tell later when the tense moments of a dangerous encounter were over. Heavy postwar boom traffic as it was, chases didn't reach terribly high speeds, and the Missouri State Highway Patrol's 90-horsepower, circa-1950 Chevrolets, Plymouths, and Fords were plenty. But occasionally, one of these cars would be pushed to the limit in pursuit of some of the more determined bad guys, as was the case when a '51 Ford patrol car chased a '51 Ford getaway car.

"Trooper Taylor and I were on 66 in Lebanon waiting for two robbers who robbed a service station and cafe west of Rolla one Sunday evening," Tinnin says. "After a while, we spotted the car and chased it through the streets

Tinnin joined the Missouri State Highway Patrol in 1949. *Missouri State Highway Patrol collection*

Tinnin worked this tragic wreck in the early 1950s. This Dodge's driver was smashed into the steering column on Route 66 3 miles east of U.S. 63 near Rolla. *Missouri State Highway Patrol collection*

Tinnin threw many a desperado into the old Lebanon, Missouri, jailhouse.

of Lebanon, making six or eight corners and leaving tire marks on all of them. Second gear was out on their car, and we could use our second gear to overtake them. The rifles in our car hung long-wise above the doors—a shotgun on the right, and a .51-caliber semiautomatic Winchester on the left. I was driving, and Trooper Taylor shot the back glass out of their car, and the passenger robber was leaning out the window firing a little pistol at us. Taylor put nine shots from the Winchester through the back of that car, and when the robbers decided to stop, they pulled over to the curb between a funeral home and the police station! Stan Palmer was the coroner and undertaker, and he came out of the funeral home and saw what was happening. I told him later, 'Stan, you had the most disappointed look on your face when you saw those two guys were still standing up!'"

Now in his late 70s, Tinnin is still patrolling America as an active RVer, grateful to be alive after a number of narrow escapes.

"I lucked out on World War II, and I lucked out on getting shot," he says. "I guess the good Lord wants me around for some reason."

TOM PASLEY— MISSOURI STATE HIGHWAY PATROL

Tom Pasley is a big man with a big, low voice. His speech may be slow, gentle, and permeated with central Missouri friendliness, but to an evildoer, Pasley's voice was no doubt a booming expression of authority when he was in the uniform of a Missouri trooper. This authority led him to a 33-year career as a trooper and his election as Phelps County Sheriff, a position that lasted 16 years. Along the way, Pasley contributed an enduring image of the Missouri State Highway Patrol logo to the citizens of the Show Me State and to the travelers passing through.

Pasley was born in 1915 in Calaway County, north of Jefferson City. His interests led him to study for an art degree at the Southeast State Teachers College in Cape Girardeau, but other interests led him to join the highway patrol in 1939. He was trained at Camp Hawthorn near Lake of the Ozarks where recruits slept in screen-sided cabins and the water would freeze in the fire buckets on the cold November nights. His first assignment was to Troop C in St. Louis, where his patrol area covered Route 66 through the suburb of Kirkwood.

He joined the Marine Corps for World War II, and upon his return was assigned in rapid succession to Troop F in Camdenton and then to Troop I in the 66 town of Rolla in the steep grades, sharp curves, and sometimes cold and icy weather of the Ozark Mountains.

Pasley's artistic talents got noticed and put to use while he worked in Camdenton in September 1946.

"The colonel called down there one day saying they were getting complaints that the troopers weren't getting seen and told me he wanted me to design an emblem that could be seen, and I designed it and took it to him the next day," Pasley recalls, adding that the project went from concept to finished product in a single evening. "Then, I designed the emblem on the motorcycles for the Safety Squadron, and I traveled all over the state and painted numbers on top of the patrol cars."

This logo was an immediate success and has been used unchanged on Missouri State Highway Patrol cars ever since.

The highway patrol also created a unique concept in highway policing in 1940—the Safety Squadron. Made up of 13 troopers, which included Pasley, the squadron rode gleaming white, chrome-dripping, extra-fancy, meant-to-be-seen Harley-Davidson motorcycles, and their duties included working special traffic details all over Missouri like the state fair or anticipated holiday traffic. They also participated in parades, sometimes as far away as California. Much of the time, however, the Safety Squadron worked various sections of highway intensely where its job was to be the "good cops" who pulled motorists over not to ticket them but to warn them of bald tires, cracked lenses, or road hazards ahead. They would help people in need and be the cops the tax-paying public was glad to see.

When trouble hit, however, and the Safety Squadron was nearby, they were pressed into action as they were one evening while working Route 66 near Joplin.

"We had worked a 12-hour day on the motorcycles, and we were coming in for the evening," Pasley remembers. "An officer by the name of Potts drove up on a car to check it, and the fellow leaned out the window and shot Potts with a shotgun. Only a few of the pellets hit him so it didn't kill him. So they called everybody in, including all the boys on motorcycles, and we had a manhunt all the way from Joplin to Baxter Springs [Kansas]. I was the only one who didn't get into a car because we didn't have enough cars. I stayed out all night on the motorcycle. Potts and another trooper named Grammar were in a car, and they came down a country road, and there was a log across the road. Grammar got out to move the log, and he got shot in the back end with a shotgun. The [bad guys] were laying in a ditch because their car had broken down or something. Now, the manhunt was on foot, and I was out in Kansas on that little old motorcycle. It was a foggy morning with a lot of dew on the ground, and I saw a light coming across the field. Of course, it startled me, and I was hiding behind my motorcycle with my gun drawn. It turned out to be two old farmers. One of the [bad guys] had gone in and tried to rob a farmer of his car, and these farmers jumped him. They tied him up with barbed wire around his wrists! Later, when I was an instructor at the school, I told all my recruits that if they ran out of handcuffs, they could just go get some barbed wire."

Every police officer's career is filled with accidents, and some have humorous conclusions. Pasley had gotten a call that there was a wreck west of Rolla in the town of Doolittle in front of the T&T Restaurant.

"It was early in the morning, and I looked all over. I called in and said, 'There's no wreck out here,' and they said, 'There's got to be a wreck out there.' There used to be a little old church that sat down here, and [after passing it a few times] I thought the church looked a little funny. These soldiers had run across this intersection, and they were sitting in their car, inside the church, up against the pulpit, drunker than hell. They had driven *clear inside*!"

Other accidents had very unfunny conclusions, made far more tragic by the fact they could have been prevented.

"I got a call [about a traffic hazard] out east of Rolla on old 66, and when I got out there, there was a tractor-trailer parked in the road," he says. "It was a dark night, and I asked the truck driver why he was parked on the road, and he said, 'Officer, I don't know. My truck just

Tom Pasley, 1946. The Missouri State Highway Patrol discovered he had been an art student, and asked him to design the department's official logo. *Missouri State Highway Patrol collection*

Tom Pasley, 1999. There's no need to change something good, and Pasley and his logo are still seen on Route 66 in Rolla.

Gene Tinnin shows off Pasley's logo on this 1959 Dodge patrol car.

gotten drunk, and when they got to St. James, the driver decided he was going to drive with his lights out, and that truck driver was telling me the absolute truth about not seeing what happened. This [living soldier] couldn't believe how lucky he was. He got out at St. James because he wasn't going to ride with them if they were going to run with their lights out."

The unpleasant is always a part of a cop's life, but the humorous is remembered better, as with Pasley's cartoon character case in the early 1950s.

"I had been rasslin' with a mouthy, fighting drunk one day, and even after taking him to jail, I wasn't too happy. Rasslin' around with him had knocked me around pretty good and gotten my uniform all dirty. I was still mad as hell later when I saw a car with Pennsylvania license plates that I thought I'd better check out. The driver of the car was a guy about 30, and I asked him his name, and he told me his name was Donald Duck! Well, I was in no mood for jokes, and I got mad and yelled at him, but then he showed me his driver's license, and there it was. His name really was Donald J. Duck!"

West of Rolla, on 66's approach to the Little Piney River, stands Beacon Hill, so named for the flashing beacon that used to guide airplanes safely through the Ozarks. To motorists, truck drivers, and troopers, Beacon Hill had a different meaning—white knuckles. To the westbound 66 traveler, Beacon Hill meant careening downhill toward two sudden curves before reaching the narrow, now-gone bridge over the river, and to the eastbound traveler, it meant a long, slow climb with trucks pulling the hill at a snail's pace. It was a scene made for state troopers, and during one violent, bitterly icy snowstorm in the early 1960s, Pasley and his fellow men in blue were needed.

"I spent days and nights out at Beacon Hill," Pasley says. "They'd slide down that hill, and they couldn't get up the other side, and it got all jammed. For two days one whole night, I was out there. The road graders would clear

stopped.' I kind of got suspicious. The flatbed trailer had huge blocks of marble on it, and I walked around to the back of the trailer, and there was a Buick that had run clear under that trailer, and there were soldiers dead in it. What made it [even more suspicious] was that the trucker said he didn't see anything happen and that his truck had just stopped on its own. Pretty soon a car drove up, and another soldier got out, and he came running up screamin' and hollerin', 'Those are my buddies, those are my buddies!' He said they'd all been to St. Louis and

While working one of the common wrecks on the narrow Beaver Creek bridge west of Rolla in the late 1950s, a motorist stopped to tell Tom Pasley about another wreck that had just occurred down the road. As proof, the motorist showed Pasley a photograph of the wreck. This was the first time Pasley had seen an instant Polaroid photo.

the road up to the top of the hill, and by the time they got turned around and started back, it was terrible again."

Pasley took freezing motorists with marooned vehicles back to restaurants to get them out of the cold. There were so many major accidents that troopers were barely able to get to the minor ones.

But the bad times of snowstorms on Beacon Hill's section of 66 passed with the coming of Interstate 44 and the demolition of the Little Piney River bridge. The good times of being a cop during a less threatening time passed as well, but we still have the stories of cops like Tom Pasley—brave men who don't brag about it.

CLYDE McCUNE— COP, JUDGE, MERCHANT, AND TOWN FOUNDER

Clyde McCune isn't a tall man, but he walked the walk of a very big man as he faced personal losses, founded a town, policed a highway, and performed as a judge.

McCune was born in the spring of 1918 in Glenville, Nebraska. He served in the Army Air Corp as a test pilot during World War II.

"I did engineering tests. I flew the big ones—B-17s, B-24s, C-47s . . . ," McCune tells. "I didn't fly any combat at all. I never had anybody shooting at my tail feathers, and I was damn glad of it too!"

Flying was in McCune's blood, but his young wife was diagnosed with a serious illness in 1946, and doctors told McCune that she would have to live in a warm, dry climate. They specifically recommended Kingman, Arizona, where McCune quickly found work in the electrical industry.

The 90-mile loop of rural Route 66 extending between Kingman and Seligman is one of the most popular and heavily visited sections of the highway traveled by modern Route 66 enthusiasts. Kingman is the site of the annual Route 66 Fun Run car show and celebration, and Seligman is home to Juan and Angel Delgadillo—notables among the originators of the modern Route 66 nostalgia movement. Scattered between these towns are smaller towns rich with roadside interest—Hackberry, former home to Route 66 artist and collectible creator Bob Waldmire; Valentine, site of the imposing and beautiful former Indian school building; the topographically beautiful and foliated Crozier Canyon Ranch; and Peach Springs, seat of the Hualapai Indian Reservation.

Tom Pasley worked a wreck in 1951 involving this '37 Buick. *Missouri State Highway Patrol collection*

In the high flat valley between Crozier Canyon and Peach Springs sits demure, solitary Truxton. Approaching from either direction, a weary driver came over a rise and gazed down an 8-mile stretch of highway, seeing every inch of it, making the isolation of the Arizona wilderness that the Mother Road crossed real to him.

"The Department of the Interior had been talking about building a dam across the Colorado River at Bridge Canyon, and the reasonable way to get to that from Highway 66 was the take-off there from Truxton," McCune explains. "The road would have gone up to the reservation and then taken what we call the Buck and Doe Road out to the canyon. That's the reason we set up our business there in 1950. It was called Truxton Garage. Then, they changed their minds and didn't build the dam, and consequently, Truxton didn't get very big, but we were still there. Don Dilts was building his little restaurant and service station contemporarily with my garage, so he and I

Northwestern Arizona was still the Wild West when Clyde McCune (left) began cleaning up the towns as a Mohave County sheriff's deputy. With McCune is Deputy Ray Baily in a photo taken in 1962. *Clyde McCune collection*

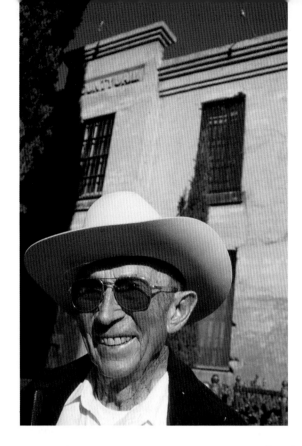

Wearing the same hat in the new century that he wore in the 1962 photo, Clyde McCune pays a visit to the old jailhouse in Kingman where he threw many a bad guy as both a deputy and judge.

were the beginners. Dilts was an inspector on the Santa Fe tracks, and his wife and one son ran the cafe in Truxton. The area was called Truxton when we got there because I think it was named for Truxton Canyon, which headed out from there about 6 or 7 miles to the west. My shop is completely demolished now. The fellow I sold it to leased it to the state, and they kept their road construction crews and other things in there. One day, they had one hell of a storm, and lightening hit this thing and burned the roof. The walls came down, and all in all, it was a mess so they just bulldozed it all."

McCune is modest about having founded a modest town, but any town still standing on Route 66 that saw the road's heyday and fall is filled with history, and thankfully in the case of Truxton, the world still has McCune to attest to the town's foundations. Thanks to McCune and Dilts, others followed.

The story of McCune's life takes a turn in 1952 after he sold the Truxton Garage. After a brief stay with the Truxton Canyon Indian Agency running one of their trading posts, McCune found himself joining the Mohave County Sheriff's Department in 1953 in an on-call capacity and going full-time as a deputy working out of the Kingman office in 1956. Here begin the stories of taming what was still, in some ways, the Old West.

"There were quite a number of serious automobile accidents on 66," McCune says. "The first one I ever handled as a deputy was just a little bit west of Peach Springs. It was a head-on collision with nine people in the one car—people from the sawmill up in Peach Springs—and there were three people in the other car, and two of them were killed. I almost turned in my badge right then. It was pretty rough. Really, the first accident I ever handled was

also the most serious accident I ever handled. Eleven people were killed in that one. There was only one survivor—a poor little old Mexican man. He was wandering around there saying, 'My whole family. I've lost my whole family.' It was a shame. You had to be careful. There was enough traffic that if you started to pass, you had better know where you were going and get the passing done before you went head-on with something."

Accidents weren't the only concern for a cop. Route 66 was a favorite among criminals on the lamb.

"Stolen cars! They called Kingman the stolen car capital of the world. We had the checking stations on Highways 66 and 93 both, and they'd spot these kids who had stolen cars there. The inspectors got to where they were pretty good at spotting them, and they would just radio in and tell us to stop such-and-such a car because they thought it was stolen. Sometimes, the kids didn't fit the car, and sometimes the inspectors would see a license plate wired on. A lot of the time, what they saw was just a really nice car that didn't fit the driver. Sometimes, they would see there was no luggage—little things like that."

When it's time for the former policeman to tell his stories to his grandchildren, one can bet the chases are going to be at the top of the list.

"I was riding with the sheriff, and I don't remember why we wanted to pull this car over, but I think it was a stolen car. The minute they realized we were going to try to stop them, they really stomped on that thing. It was a brand-new Oldsmobile—about a '57 or '58 model. We were driving a '57 Chevy with a police [engine and suspension] package on it, and that thing would really fly. We were out east of town on 66—out in that long, flat area—and the old sheriff wouldn't let up on the Olds. He kept crowding them just a little. All at once, they lost control of that stolen car, and they flipped it. I remember looking out the passenger's side window of our police car and seeing the *underside* of that Oldsmobile. It just went straight on up in the air, and we went right on past them. It just went end over end. You know, those two kids weren't hurt. I don't know how it didn't kill them, but it didn't. They got out and took off on the run. I put a few shots from my 30-30 into the dirt near them, and they decided to stop running."

McCune's career is filled with the wild stories—truths stranger and more violent than fiction. After serving as a sheriff's deputy, McCune served as justice of the peace and magistrate and was known for holding criminals' feet to the

McCune and the Dilts family were the first to build their businesses at the location of a proposed crossroads east of Peach Springs—thus, founding the town of Truxton, Arizona.

fire while giving young men who needed a second chance plenty of leash to try a better life.

Whether talking about a shoot-out in Valentine, bar fights in Hackberry, car chases through Kingman, wild curves through Oatman, or head-on collisions everywhere, McCune agrees that Arizona sounds like the Wild West clear into the 1950s, but McCune also had a hand in settling the Old West by bringing civilization to Truxton and justice to Mohave County.

SERGEANT BUZZ BANKS— CALIFORNIA HIGHWAY PATROL

There was no Route 66 on November 21, 1913, but there was a new baby boy in Los Angeles, California, named Lewellen Banks. Later nicknamed Buzz, he felt the Mojave Desert's call.

"You could call me a native Los Angelino, but at the same time, I hated L.A. with a purple passion as far as living in it is concerned," says Banks, whose way out of the big city was to join the California Highway Patrol (CHP) in 1941 at age 27—a decision which also gave him the "certain extent of excitement and adventure" he was looking for and a home in Route 66's desert town of Victorville. Excitement and adventure are certainly found in Banks' 1994 book *Policing the Old Mojave*.

Within months of Banks' joining the CHP, the Japanese bombed Pearl Harbor, and the United States was at war. German Field Marshall Rommel was raising Cain in northern Africa, and it would soon be up to U.S. General George Patton to help fight off Rommel's hoards of Panzer tanks with American tank soldiers trained in the Mojave Desert. It would be up to Banks to help escort the military troops through his territory safely.

"General Patton stopped off at the old sheriff's office on Seventh Street [66]," Banks remembers. "He pulled up on the wrong side of the street, which was all right because he was part of a military convoy. He strides up to the sheriff's office on the west side of the street and asked for directions. He was wearing his pearl-handled revolvers and his tall motorcycle-riding-type boots with his pants tucked in them. He talked in

the sheriff's office for maybe two minutes, and he walks out—strides out, literally—hops into his Jeep, and away they go."

Banks remembers Patton's convoys taking rather long, strange routes through the desert, possibly due to fears of being spied upon, and there were precautions required of Banks as well.

"We had to be careful. We couldn't use the radios much. We had orders to operate with our headlights off. We even had to shield our red taillight lenses. You could fly over the desert for years after the war and see tank tracks all over the place."

When leaving 1940s Los Angeles for points east on Route 66, one would drive east through the intermittent countryside between L.A. and San Bernardino. Here 66 made a hard left turn north to begin the climb up the treacherous Cajon Pass over the San Bernardino Mountains—a long, steep, winding road where big trucks routinely progressed at a literal walking pace. Once finally reaching the Cajon Summit at more than 4,000 feet, the Mojave Desert began, and it was a long, gentle slope all the way to Victorville 15 miles later and nearly 2,000 feet lower. Today, this drive takes less than two hours on Interstates 10 and 15. In the 1940s and 1950s, this could take all day on two-lane Route 66, which made Victorville a shining example of 66's roadside culture. It was alive with motels, eateries, garages, and gas stations needed by road-weary travelers and truckers. Victorville's Seventh Street and D Street were home to Route 66. U.S. Highways 66, 91, and 395 all merged in San Bernardino for the Cajon climb, and once over the summit and into the desert, 395 broke off and headed due north toward California's Sierra Nevada Mountains, and 91 broke off in Barstow and headed for Las Vegas, Nevada, and Salt Lake City, Utah.

World War II ended, and the Mojave Desert was quickly back to better-than-normal as postwar prosperity hit. Route 66 became busier and busier as Las Vegas-bound tourist traffic increased, and with this increase, 66 came to have, in Banks' words, "a load of undesirable people driving on it." The patrolmen called it "dude traffic," and it contained all the elements of old Las Vegas—sinners and mafiosi.

"We probably had more criminals running down Route 66 than any other highway in the United States," Banks says.

California Highway Patrolman Buzz Banks smiles at being in the presence of a 1955 Buick patrol car. Banks escorted General Patton's tank convoys down Route 66 through the Mojave Desert during World War II. Gary Goltz has restored this 1955 Buick into an accurate recreation of the patrol car driven by actor Broderick Crawford in the 1950s TV hit, "Highway Patrol." Goltz patrols his classic on Route 66 through his hometown of Upland, California.

Buzz Banks, circa 1940.

They ran, but Banks caught them.

"We did have car pursuits off and on, but they became more common after the war. I'm not sure what to ascribe it to, but seemed like [criminals] had that notion they were God, and by golly, they were not going to let themselves be caught and prosecuted. Pursuits here on the north side of the Cajon Pass didn't generally last too long because we'd be able to knock them down by the time they got to Victorville. [The bad guys] just couldn't risk going through town maintaining that kind of speed.

"One of the toughest pursuits I ever had started out in Baker on old 91 westbound into Barstow where I picked it up, and then they headed out east toward Needles on 66," he tells. "It was two guys in a stolen car. [Banks believes it was a 1957 Dodge.] We had several officers join the chase, but some had to drop out for gasoline reasons. We chased them all the way out to Amboy [80 miles]. We set up a roadblock that probably would have killed them. I was the sergeant, and my duty was to control this thing."

Buzz called ahead by radio and set up a scheme involving a semitrailer backing out onto the road to stop the bad guys.

"The [bad guy] got a hunch and whipped over to the side of the road and hit his brakes, and by that time, I was up really close to him, and I had to slam on my binders to keep from hitting him. I still bumped his bumper. Both of them jumped out and ran."

Banks laughs as he remembers these desperadoes jumping out and running away from the police in Amboy—the harshest desert on all of 66.

"They wouldn't have gotten far!"

Banks agrees that as cars got faster in the 1950s, people did dumber things to pass the trucks.

"[The 1950s marked] the transition from sensible driving to nonsensical driving. People got more power behind the wheel, and they weren't used to it, but they drove like they'd always had it."

Some groups gain bad reputations because of the reputation of a few members, and Banks says "9 out of 10" gas stations and garages along 66 through the Mojave were honest, but there was always that 10 percent.

"They would do petty things you wouldn't think a grown man would think of like setting his gasoline meter so it read one-tenth of a gallon more than what it was delivering. Some of them got a lot worse. They were cheating on fan belts and radiator hoses—stuff that could run into some money—by cutting them or jerking them loose."

Even at stations owned by honest people, some employees would sell parts unnecessarily to motorists and pocket the money unknown to the honest owners. The farther out in the desert, the worse it got.

Nature threw difficulties at all drivers who traveled 66 through the Mojave. The Cajon Pass snows in solidly in the winter, and Amboy can reach 120 degrees in the summer. When the Cajon Pass iced over in the winter, Banks says most of the garage owners who went to the pass to gouge motorists on snow chains weren't local.

"[Amboy's heat gave motorists a lot of trouble] because they didn't know how to drive to keep their cars cool," Banks says. "They'd turn on the air conditioning and poke along [and overheat in the middle of nowhere]. They needed to turn off the air conditioning and rev up the rpm of the engine by driving in second gear if they had to. It was a lack of knowledge on the part of people, by and large."

Route 66 had its dangers: the Cajon Pass and Amboy and the surprise of finding the narrow Oro Grande Bridge over the Mojave River north of Victorville, the tight S-curve under the railroad tracks in the town of Oro Grande, and the curves through the hills halfway between Victorville and Barstow near the town of Helendale. But Buzz Banks helped keep it safe, and his book, *Policing the Old Mojave* has helped keep Route 66 in the minds of younger people.

"Once the newspaper reporters and televisions start humming away about 66, [younger people] start asking, 'Well, what was 66?' It has so many nostalgic memories—more so than any other highway coming into the West," he says. "Sixty-six nudges the older people, and the [younger people notice and wonder why]."

PAT MATLACH'S DESERT MOTORS, VICTORVILLE, CALIFORNIA

In the world of Route 66 nostalgia, it seems forgotten that neon wasn't always revered as a cultural icon, and gritty novels and Rod Serling scripts recount the underside of the neon jungle where blazing tubes meant blaring sleaze and crass shouting. With the passing of the neon era, however, Americans quickly realized the artistry and character of these signage masterpieces. Seldom were any two alike, and while they may have been annoying when screaming at 66 motorists in groups of 30-in-a-row on every town's Main Street, their shining, flashing individuality speaks to modern nostalgists who crave a break in today's sameness.

World War II made owning a car just a little difficult with fuel, tire, and oil rations taking their tolls on the condition and usefulness of the average family car. In 1945, one kid turned this to his advantage and made a career of providing cars along Route 66 and providing nostalgists in the post-66 era with some of the best preserved, most authentic roadside neon to be seen anywhere.

Pat Matlach delivered newspapers to the entire burg of Milstadt, Illinois, and noticed a lot of cars sitting in garages waiting for World War II to run it course. The cars could be had for a song during the war because farm trucks had much bigger rations of fuel than passenger cars, and the enterprising young man began buying the cars in rural Illinois and selling them at substantial profits in the metropolis of St. Louis, Missouri.

At one point, Matlach picked up a low-mileage 1936 Ford in Illinois, took it over the river to St. Louis and ran ads in two newspapers. When he received nearly 300 phone calls from prospective buyers for this single, austere economy car, Matlach knew what business to go into and where. At age 17, he went to work in a dealership in St. Louis, and by age 19, he owned his own used car lot at 4955 Natural Bridge Avenue, half a block east of King's Highway. Though not very close to Route 66's incarnation as Gravois Avenue, St. Louis was still a 66 town, and the highway was important to his business.

"I handled off-breeds, and by that I mean Packards, Studebakers, Hudsons, Hupmobiles—different cars other than Fords, Chevys, and Plymouths," Matlach explains. "If I got a nice '41 Chevy club coupe, I could take it out in the country and trade it for a half a dozen off-breeds at a Chevrolet dealer in, say, Rolla, Missouri. We'd go over into Illinois and do the same thing. I had a fairly small business in St. Louis, and I was in the middle of a lot of used car lots, and I didn't have a lot of money or a very big lot so handling the off-breeds was a niche market instead of handling the Fords, Chevys, Oldsmobiles, and other things that were popular."

Liking airplanes, Matlach joined the Air National Guard. The Korean War sent him to active duty in 1951 at George Air Force Base in Victorville, California. It was a smallish 66 town at the western gateway to the harsh

Pat Matlach of Desert Motors has been selling cars on Route 66 from the same location for nearly a half-century.

Mojave Desert, 15 miles north of the Cajon Pass, the treacherous, steep, winding, cold/hot door between the San Bernardino and San Gabriel Mountains. The pass presented Matlach with all its perils as his seven-day trip to California from a military base in Texas reached its conclusion.

"I made the mistake of not coming on 66," he says. "I came the southern route because I thought I'd be on more flat ground than if I had gone through Albuquerque and over the Continental Divide and so on. This Cadillac was very low mileage, being one of those '42s that wasn't sold until '45, and it only had about 40,000 miles on it. It had a very low-pressure radiator cap, but I found a Mack truck pressure cap that helped it quite a bit."

After a harrowing, heat-intensive trip through western Arizona and into California, the seven-day trip was only going to get worse as Matlach, his wife, their newborn son, and their Cadillac joined Route 66 for the ride of a lifetime up the Cajon Pass pulling a 43-foot mobile home in late-July heat with blocks of ice on the Cadillac's floor and two water coolers in the windows.

"[Route 66] up the Cajon Pass was just a two-lane road in those days," Matlach recalls. "All the way up, there would be one truck doing 8 miles per hour and

another truck doing 9 miles per hour trying to pass him, and we would have to stop all the time to let the Cadillac cool down. One place I had to stop was by a railroad trestle, and I had a three-wheel hydraulic dolly that I was using to pull the trailer. I couldn't get going because the wheels were spinning. We were in the gravel, and the trailer was so heavy, we couldn't get traction. I had to go back and crank a lot more weight down on the rear of the Cadillac so I could get started. It took us from one o'clock in the afternoon to nine o'clock at night to get from San Bernardino to Victorville, and most of that was done about a half a mile at a time because of stopping to let the Cadillac cool down. The original Cajon Summit went up to over 4,400 feet, and up at the old Summit Inn, there were water barrels for people to replenish their radiators from overheating coming up. In the wintertime when it was cold and snowing, you'd walk into the old Summit Inn, and there was a massive fireplace which was very welcoming."

Despite thinking he would only be in Victorville for a short time, 21-year-old Matlach was soon back in the used car business employing the same off-breed strategies that made him successful in St. Louis. He struck a deal with the owner of Bud's Garage on the west side of Victorville's section of 66, which occupied D Street. Matlach opened Desert Motors for business and experienced immediate success.

There were bluffs to the west of Matlach's lot, and there was a natural cut in those bluffs which allowed the sun to shine on Desert Motors long after the hills had cast their evening shadows over the rest of D Street. This made Desert Motors a shining place clear until dark, but this advantage became the undoing of Desert Motors' first location. This cut in the hill that shined for Pat Matlach was like a flashlight showing the highway department where to put a freeway. In the fall of 1953, the surveying started, and in January 1954, condemnation proceedings started against property in the path of the new superhighway. Fortunately, in 1952, Matlach had bought a diesel repair shop and Mobil gas station on the other side of the street and just a little to the south, creating a ready-made new home for Desert Motors, which opened in this location in April 1954.

The new location took on that neon-era glow with a bright turquoise-and-white paint job, strings of clear-glass light bulbs shining points of light on glossy waxed cars

Matlach still uses the rarely seen clear-glass bulbs over the lot at Desert Motors. Car dealers used to call it "the instant polish job."

at night, and dripping from it all, was Desert Motors' exceptional abundance of beautiful neon.

"When I opened up here, I was the only used car lot in town," Matlach says. "The new car dealers in those days did not really do a lot of business in low-priced transportation cars. They sold some late-model used cars, but not many. I put good quality, low-priced transportation cars on the lot, and I had people coming in from all over. We ran a small radio ad in Barstow because there was no radio station in Victorville, and half of our business was from the Barstow area. In 1953 and '54 I sold over 600 cars a year off the old lot. Everybody from Chicago to Santa Monica passed my door. I had the biggest used car lot between Albuquerque and San Bernardino on Route 66. The fact that I was so successful here, I think, is the reason other car dealers opened up here, because we were known. We sold cars to people who came our way, and we sold cars to people who broke down. Coming up the Cajon Pass on a hot afternoon in those days, there would be a lot of cars overheating, rods going out, and radiators going bad. We had a service garage, and we were open 24 hours per day, Thursday through Sunday."

The first bypass of downtown Victorville was opened in 1956, missing Desert Motors by very little, but it was enough in spite of cars still spilling out onto D Street to continue their trip to Barstow on 66. In 1959, the freeway was completed to Barstow, and eastbound travelers could then drive from San Bernardino all the way to Barstow without ever getting onto the old two-lane portions of 66.

"[The first bypass] cut our business in half because all the Barstow traffic didn't pass my door anymore," he explains. "So, what we did was start selling a more expensive vehicle that made a bigger profit instead of the volume we had been doing. We never again sold 600 cars a year. In '53 we sold almost 700, and in '54 we sold 600 cars, but after that, we sold substantially less, but we made more money. [When the second bypass happened] I think we actually got more traffic then because people were on the freeway for a while, and this was a natural place to stop, and it actually increased our business. With the freeway going all the way to Needles, Victorville became more of a halfway point, and a lot of people came into town off [the D Street and Palmdale Road exits] because Route 66 was the business loop through town that people were ready

for by the time they got this far. After the first bypass, it was still two-lane road all the way here from Barstow, and the last thing they wanted was more two-lane road through town, and when they saw that freeway, they got on it, and they were gone. But when it became freeway all the way, they were ready for a town."

As for driving 66 himself?

"I always drove the big cars. I always had a Cadillac or hemi [hemispherical combustion chamber] Chrysler. The Chrysler power steering was so touchy in those days that I kind of preferred the Cadillacs. I remember I had a Hudson Hornet with a Borg-Warner overdrive transmission and power steering—fantastic car! I loved that Hudson because it handled so good. [Route 66] was dangerous because on the flat areas, people did some speeding. I was one of them. I had a bet with Scotty who owned Scott's Cafe [which fronted 66 near today's California Route 66 Museum]. Scott had a 1952 Chrysler hemi New Yorker, and I had a 1953 Jaguar Roadster—the one used in the movie *Angel Face* with Robert Mitchum. This was a souped-up roadster, and Scotty and I had a bet that I could leave here and pull into the Harris department store on E Street in San Bernardino [about 50 miles] in 30 minutes. I won the bet! I drove down that two-lane road through the Cajon Pass at speeds of over 100 miles per hour in places, and from [Victorville] to the

Looking south at the old Cajon Pass Summit, now bypassed on each side by the much lower lanes of Interstate 15. On the left is the 1920s alignment, and on the right is the postwar alignment where Pat Matlach once won a bet by driving his '53 Jaguar down the pass at 100 miles per hour and where Bill Pierce used to struggle to crest the hill as a trucker with a load of new cars.

Cajon Summit at speeds well over 100 miles per hour. The sad story is later, Scotty ran that Chrysler under a truck and got killed. There was only about 6 feet of that Chrysler sticking out from under that truck, and the speedometer was stuck at 110 miles per hour. It happened on 66, just this side of the Summit."

The neon era came and went, and as the 1960s and 1970s moved on into the 1980s, Desert Motors had its ups and downs with the gas crunch, economic roller coasters, and the closing of the nearby George Air Force Base. As the 1990s came and went, Route 66 achieved its place as a cultural icon. Pat Matlach, approaching his 70s, has reached somewhat heroic status for having weathered these ups and downs and preserved some of the Mother Road's finest neon for the future. As long as there's a dollar to be made selling used cars, there's a chance for Desert Motors to not be an exhibit in a museum but, rather, a genuine, working piece of neon culture with bragging rights about having never really gone away.

BILL PIERCE— ROUTE 66 TRUCK DRIVER

Bill Pierce misses working. Most people are happy to retire, but any conversation with Pierce quickly turns to his decades as a truck driver on Route 66. It's clear that if he had his way, he'd still be out there delivering new cars to dealerships six or eight at a time as a proud union car hauler.

Pierce was 22 years old in 1952 when he got his first truck-driving job hauling new Chryslers from the docks of Buffalo, New York, to the big cities of the East Coast. Needless to say, Pierce learned a lot about driving big, loaded trucks in tough winter weather, and this education would serve him well when he moved to California in 1954 and began driving trucks again in 1957 after a stint as a car salesman in Santa Monica. Like millions of other Americans, the move to California was Pierce's first exposure to U.S. Highway 66.

"When I first came out here, I took 66 out of Chicago all the way to Santa Monica," Pierce recalls. "It was a slow trip. From Buffalo to Chicago, they had the old interstates, but from Chicago to L.A., 66 was all two-lane road. I was out in the flat country—the prairie of the Midwest—and it wasn't too bad, but the further west I got, the higher the land got, and I got into mountains and winding roads. You had a lot of slow places

in the mountainous regions of New Mexico and Arizona on 66. It was hard traveling."

After a short stint driving trucks part-time for military families moving from base to base, Pierce was back to hauling cars in 1959.

"At the beginning, we just had gas rigs. We were hauling at that time a six-car maximum, and a lot of our trucks were only five-car rigs. Whether you were hauling five or six cars depended on the size of the cars. I'd pick up the cars at the Ford plant, and I'd transport them from Long Beach, California, into New Mexico as far as Albuquerque."

Why do cars run on gasoline, and why do big trucks run on diesel? The short story is that a diesel engine develops a lot of power at a low engine speed. A gasoline engine under a heavy load must be turning very fast to develop the power to pull a loaded truck over a hill, but a diesel engine can be turning much more slowly and develop plenty of power to make a heavy load fight gravity up an incline. To provide a gas engine with enough rpm to pull a vehicle up a hill, big trucks were equipped with lots and lots of low gears. Many had a four-speed transmission, a three-speed gearbox behind the transmission, and a two-speed rear axle, making for 12 to 16 gears and lots of levers for the driver to operate. A very common sight on Route 66 was a truck pulling a long hill, with all gearboxes in low gears, which drivers call "compound low," and the gasoline-fueled engine screaming wide open.

This was how the eastbound Bill Pierce negotiated the Cajon Pass north of San Bernardino, the two long pulls east of Amboy on the California side of the Colorado River, and the steep, abrupt mountains climbing up to Williams and Flagstaff on the Arizona side. Along the way were minor but difficult inconveniences like sudden steep curves north of Victorville, California, and a long steady climb up Crozier Canyon east of Kingman, Arizona, and the tough climb into Kingman itself.

Western Arizona is the place where the modern Route 66 nostalgia movement began, and it's one of the most loved and traveled sections of the old road, but for Pierce it was his least favorite and most difficult stretch.

"Once you left Needles and headed for Flagstaff, that was a really vicious road. You'd be going down the road, and you'd come around a curve, and there'd be a disabled car or truck sitting there. [It was scary] especially if there was traffic coming the other way. That caused a lot of accidents. A lot of drivers at that time would not try to get off the road. They would just stay there in the middle of the road disabled. In some places, there was no room to get off the road, but in other places they could have gotten over some, and anything would have helped if they had just moved over a little because the roads weren't that wide."

Having braved some difficulties to get there, Albuquerque then presented its obstacles with its high summer heat, low winter cold, and a long, steady climb that goes on for miles.

"You had a passing lane," Pierce explains. "Mostly, it was cars doing the passing. It didn't matter what kind of truck you had, they were all geared about the same, and they would be climbing through Albuquerque at 10 or 12 miles per hour in compound-low with the engine wide open. The only ones that were going faster were empty, but otherwise all the trucks climbing through were in one long line."

Of course, heading back west to California forced Pierce and everyone else to drive down these mountains, which introduced a whole new set of gravity-fighting problems.

"You had to come down in a low gear to help your brakes. The Cajon Pass was really bad to come down," he says. "You had some really bad curves on the Cajon Pass. Flagstaff had some beauties too. I was lucky that it never happened in front of my eyes, but I had run across many wrecks where cars and trucks had gone over the side of the road on these hills and, in some cases, dropped straight down hundreds of feet and hit bottom. In the mid-'60s, I had a couple of chains that broke in Arizona coming down a hill out of Kingman. I was westbound, and I was on dry pavement. There was an accident around a curve that I couldn't see until I just about ran into it. I had to throw my brakes on really, really heavy, and that caused two cars to pull forward. A couple of the chains broke, and two of the cars came together on the top deck. It caused quite a bit of damage to one of the cars where it hit the back of the car in front of it."

Heat and cold are the staples of the Southwest for the truck driver, and Pierce had his share.

"In the summertime when we knew we'd have to be coming across 66, we'd leave at about midnight so we could go over the Cajon Pass before the heat set in. Otherwise, we'd boil over. If you got there at midday,

the heat [in Amboy and Needles] was really bad, and it was hard traveling—especially with a truck with a real heavy load on it. We had small engines in the trucks at that time, and that's why we traveled at night.

"In the winter we had a hard time coming up the Cajon Pass. If it was snowing deep, they'd shut this highway down, and I was trapped up there a couple of times, but I was trapped even more in parts of New Mexico and Arizona. Many times when I was driving truck, I'd get into certain places like Williams, Arizona, or even around Albuquerque, and the snow would come. Especially between Kingman and Flagstaff, the snow would really fly bad, and they'd close the highway down, and I'd be there for two or three days in a motel. In western Arizona, you're anywhere from 5,000 to nearly 8,000 feet high, and when you had snow there in the wintertime, you had a lot of wind. The snow would be drifting across the road, and you didn't know where the road was up ahead of you. You couldn't tell when you were in the wide open spaces just where the highway was."

Weather wasn't the only danger for a trucker. Many times, a professional driver's life would be endangered by motorists whose impatience would get the better of them having been trapped behind a truck for a while.

"[Motorists] were coming off a long stretch of two-lane road that was very dangerous [between Flagstaff and Kingman] where they had to be very careful and

Most people are happy to retire, but Bill Pierce clearly misses his job as a car-hauling truck driver on Route 66.

drive slowly and cautiously, but the highway south of Kingman was wider and more wide open, and the drivers of cars just went out of their minds, really," Pierce explains. "Where the speed limit was 50 miles an hour at the time, the cars were happy doing 75 or 80 miles an hour. They were overly taking advantage of their rights. They were going too fast to control what they were doing, and it was also a bad place for people falling asleep at the wheel. When Ford came out with the fast little Thunderbird, people used to buy those little T-birds and go wild. They must have thought they had a little airplane. They just flew all over the place. They made a trucker's life hard. Heck, they made everyone's life hard. Even the pedestrians would suffer. Whenever I saw a T-bird, I expected the worst."

Pierce's own truck once caused a traffic incident of its own, though.

"In the early 1960s, I had stopped to unload some cars at the Ford dealer in Needles right on 66. At that time, the engine had to be running because we had hydraulic lifts [that operated off pumps on the truck's engine]. I put the hoist up and started unloading from the bottom. I took a car off and brought it onto the dealer's lot. I walked back, and my truck was gone. Pretty soon, I saw my truck coming back with someone driving it. What had happened was that the brakes had bled off. There was a leak in the brake system, and the truck started rolling down the highway. There was a local milkman making deliveries, and he saw the truck coming down the road. It had just missed some parked cars, and he jumped in it and took it further down the street where he could turn around and brought it back. It surprised me to death—no accidents, no damage, and no one hurt! That milkman saved the day. I'd say the truck had to have gone at least a quarter- to half-a-mile down the street before he grabbed it. It had hit a sidewalk at one point and come back to the middle of the street. Thank goodness it was just a little bit of an incline. It wasn't steep at all, otherwise it would have run away and turned over. Talk about luck! Thank goodness that milkman had enough fortitude to know what to do. A lot of people were lucky that day."

Over and over, Pierce says, "I was lucky," when asked if he was ever in an accident, directly witnessed a terrible accident, had a dangerous mishap, or experienced a bad breakdown. Could decades of daily driving on Route 66 without terrible incidents really have been just luck? Pierce's "luck" was probably attributable to a lot of skill and experience that stopped trouble before it started and made him one of those truckers whom people look back on nostalgically as having been careful, friendly, and helpful on the road.

As many times as Pierce traveled 66, one would think he would be tired of it, but as a retiree who still spends a lot of time driving on long pleasure trips, he doesn't seem tired of the old highway at all.

"Most of 66 was beautiful," he says. "From one area to another it changed dramatically. It was always something different. It was always fun to travel it. Even if you had been traveling 66 for years, as you went, you'd see something you'd never really noticed before. It always made it really interesting."

DON SHUEY— TRUCKING ON MEAN 66

What was your average teenager doing in 1938? It's a safe bet most were not truck drivers at age 15. This was the year Don Shuey's father moved his family from a Los Angeles suburb to the remote desert town of Kingman, Arizona. Shuey's father was always in business for himself in one way or another, and it was at this time that he started a produce stand in Kingman. While successful, the Kingman stand was not enough to support the families of both its business partners. Within a few years, the Shuey family relocated to Needles, California, where another produce stand business became successful enough to necessitate a twice-a-week run to the Los Angeles Produce Market.

On today's interstates, a trip from Los Angeles to Kingman is an effortless six-hour cruise on Interstates 15 and 40. In 1938, however, it was not unusual for this distance to be a 12-hour horror show. California's treacherous Cajon Pass lifted the traveler out of the fertile valleys of the Los Angeles and San Bernardino areas and Arizona's Black Mountains carried the traveler out of the deep, hot Colorado River Valley to the nearly 4,000-foot Sitgreave Summit. Both grades were hot in the summer, cold in the winter, and were steep, curvy, frightening, crowded obstacles to the simple goal of traveling by rubber-tired vehicle. Between these two fun-filled hindrances is the dangerous, lonely, harsh Mojave Desert. Every trip to the Los Angeles Produce Market was a 24-hour roundtrip through these barriers.

What took up so much time on these runs?

"No power and a lot of hills," Shuey says. "Just the Cajon Pass [about 10 miles] alone took two hours—maybe more. There were other trucks going up the hills at 2 to 3 miles an hour too."

Shuey doesn't complain, though. These hardships were just the accepted norms of the time. With the bypassing of the Black Mountains in 1953 and the nearly simultaneous improvements to the Cajon Pass, the trip got a little easier, but for those 15 years, the road and its obstructions gave Shuey some great stories to tell later generations.

"My father bought a '39 Ford truck at Cook Brothers in Los Angeles," Shuey tells, "and they made up a tandem rear axle so they could haul 7 or 8 tons on it. They made the truck bigger and a little longer. It came with 8 1/4-inch-wide, 18-inch-tall tires on it—dual tires. My father said, 'Well, since I've only got 95 horsepower, maybe if I put smaller wheels on it, I'll have more pulling power.' So, that's what he did. It had a four-speed gearbox with a two-speed rear end. My dad had a water tank on top of his truck. When it would get hot, you'd just turn this little valve, and water would run down in front of the radiator."

The more things change, the more they stay the same. Today, one climbs the Cajon Pass on Interstate 15, follows the slab to Barstow, veers onto Interstate 40, and continues to the destinations 66 used to take one to, waving good-bye to 15, which continues on to Las Vegas, Nevada, and Salt Lake City, Utah. Before the interstates, one took the combined US 66–91 to Barstow where 91 hung a left at First Street to go to Vegas and 66 continued straight east on Main Street.

"At that corner in Barstow, there was a big Standard station, and that was the world's busiest gas station—people pouring in and people pouring out all the time," Shuey says. "Barstow was like Colton, California, in those days. It was a hub, and cars and trucks would stack up for miles in all directions. I missed a lot of school. My father would call my mother; my mother would call the school, and I would be out of there to meet my father around Barstow with our little 3/4-ton '41 Ford stake-bed truck. We would unload part of his load just to relieve the weight, and we'd come home together."

Shuey went to work for the Needles Trucking Company after graduating from high school in 1942.

He drove Chevrolet and GMC ton-and-a-half semi-trucks, and Shuey learned a lesson or two about hills in the Cajon Pass with one of these venerable machines.

"I remember one time I was stopped in the Cajon Pass where Highway 138 goes off to the left in a little open spot. I had about 14 tons on this little semi. I was parked on this incline, and when I went to take off, that truck just sat there and bounced! I decided I was never going to stop there again. Once I was moving, I was going to keep moving!"

Shuey says big trucks could simply not make the Black Mountain section of 66.

"I think if they were 30 foot or over, they had to go through Prescott even as late as the early fifties."

To get from Los Angeles to Kingman, big trucks had to cross the Colorado River many miles to the south on U.S. 60 through the town of Blythe, California, head northeast to Prescott, Arizona, and continue north to finally meet 66 in Ash Fork about 110 miles east of Kingman. When the Black Mountains were bypassed in 1953, this trip was shortened by nearly 200 miles one-way.

When asked how the truckers stood all this, Shuey gives an answer befitting most historical hardships: "That's just the way it was. Those were the times."

Truckers were as vulnerable as motorists to wrecks on Route 66. This one happened in 1952 near the intersection of Route 66 and Highway H between Cuba and Sullivan, Missouri, and involved a rig from Square Deal Auto Transport of Detroit. Two of the three teenagers in the Ford were killed. The square in the middle of the photo is the inside of the Ford's passenger side door pushed all the way to the driver's side of the car. *Missouri State Highway Patrol collection*

CHAPTER 4

Route 66 Museums

Route 66 was called the Main Street of America, and it was the interstate highway system's bypass of that main street that plunged many Route 66 towns into the economic despair and abandonment hated by small business people and the quaint dilapidation loved by photographers. As the highway's importance was realized in the 1990s and efforts were made to preserve its history, museums opened their doors.

Each museum has its own reasons for existence and ways of conducting business.

The Route 66 Hall of Fame in McLean, Illinois, delivers a simply presented but charming and educational surprise at no charge to the patrons of the Dixie Truckers Home.

The Oklahoma Route 66 Museum in Clinton uses state funding and master's degrees to shine an intense spotlight on Oklahoma's and Route 66's contributions to each other.

The National Route 66 Museum in Elk City, Oklahoma, is a municipal government effort taking a nationwide view of 66 and continually shaping a successful museum plaza filled with Elk City history of all kinds.

The Devil's Rope Museum in McLean, Texas, supplements other interests in barbed wire and Texas ranching history with a Route 66 display containing only authentic artifacts by the hundreds.

The California Route 66 Museum in Victorville is a true grassroots movement by property owners and volunteers to bring interest back to a weary downtown business district.

Some old Route 66 towns are in better shape than others, and some sections of the highway are more

On the inside of the curving wall is the National Route 66 Museum's homage to the drive-up diner.

world looking for their chance to see rare artifacts and photographs. The objects used to be everywhere—along the road, in diners and gas stations, on motel night stands, in campy tourist traps, and in travelers' cars and trucks. Today, many of these objects can be seen only in museums, and the museums deserve waves of credit for providing visitors with opportunities to see rare panoramic photos of the highway's heyday or reach out and work the handle on a visible gas pump.

Some artifacts, such as postcards, were produced in huge numbers and can be owned at reasonable prices by the average 66-o-phile, but authentic items like highway marker signs have gained market values thousands of dollars beyond the reach of the average collector. Neon motel signs and tourist trap statues are physically large, expensive, one-of-a-kind items that most collectors can neither afford nor display in the space of a typical living room. Rare, high-dollar, and large items can be seen only in museums; however, with some museums allowing photography, an enthusiast can own his or her own photos of the items and plan a vacation around seeing and photographing the museums and collecting the "I was there" atmosphere that motivates most interest in Route 66 memories.

The museums subsist on gift shop sales of modern Route 66 collectibles. When these shops gain success in economically depressed downtowns or bypassed stretches of highway, they become the first centers of commerce these places have seen in decades despite some of the museums being humble or alone for a time in their success. The hope for the museums in the more depressed areas is that the motel across the street will have a few more guests, and the diner will serve a few more slices of pie and cups of coffee. Maybe the independent gas station on the corner will reopen.

Heather Roulet, formerly of the Oklahoma Route 66 Museum, and volunteer leader Delbert Trew of the Devil's Rope Museum say American and foreign gift shop customers buy different things. The foreigners tend to buy more expensive items—videos, books, full-size reproduction signs—to take back to their countries. Foreign travelers want their families to experience their Route 66 vacations with them and share all the sights they've seen through the medium of higher-range gift shop items—hence, their purchases are more information-based items. Americans know the road will always

heavily traveled than others. Victorville, Elk City, Clinton, and each of the McLeans are all remarkably different towns from each other, and their museums are likewise different from each other. The museums reflect the individual habits and situations of the towns they're in—from the professional presentation of Clinton to the homespun local knowledge of Victorville and McLean, Texas, to the image-based teaching of McLean, Illinois.

Flocking to these museums by the thousands are Route 66 enthusiasts and history buffs from around the

Reputed to be the oldest continuously operated truck stop on all of Route 66, the Dixie Truckers Home in McLean, Illinois, is home to the Route 66 Hall of Fame.

be there, and small items are adequate to serve as pleasurable souvenirs, but a sense of permanence is key to foreign travelers. Foreigners save up for years to take their vacations. The one trip they make down Route 66 may literally be their only chance to ever see it, and they will buy more permanent items. They will buy the bigger signs when they have a choice, and they will buy a leather jacket rather than nylon.

Whether American or foreign, whether collector with means or collector on a budget, whether older person with firsthand memories or young person with curiosity, the varied Route 66 museums give the visitors pleasant, educational experiences, artifacts to study, items to collect and give, and a lot of good conversation.

ROUTE 66 HALL OF FAME OF ILLINOIS

"Part of the charm of the Hall of Fame is that it's not a Las Vegas pyramid-type of thing," says Tom Teague, caretaker of the Route 66 Hall of Fame of Illinois and author of the 1991 book *Searching for 66.*

"It's not Disney World. It's humble by museum standards, and most of its visitors don't walk into the Dixie looking for it. Its humbleness puts it very much in character with the road and the nature of travel along 66. Route 66 was a road of small spontaneous pleasures—things

you just happened on. They're really neat things, but they're on a smaller scale like Stanley Marsh's Cadillac Ranch, any of the old restaurants along the way, or a Meremec Caverns sign on a barn. The little, idiosyncratic pleasures along the road are what gave it such special character. We didn't set out to encapsulate the significance of the road. We just wanted to honor the people who have something there for the visitors to see, and if they're visitors by chance, all the better because you're going to get a lot more visitors by chance than you are by deliberate action, and that's the way it used to be along Route 66."

In 1989, four people had a conversation in Bob Waldmire's hippie-style school bus in Illinois: Route 66 entrepreneur and Cozy Dog heir Bob Waldmire, postcard collector and "roadologist" Jeff Meyer, Meyer's wife at the time, Laura, and Tom Teague. Well-aware of the success of the Arizona Route 66 Association's Route 66 Fun Runs, the four decided Illinois needed a sanctioning organization too. One of the first things decided by the fledgling Illinois association was that in all titles produced by the group, whether the organization's name, events, locations, or museums, *Route 66* would always be the first words because as Teague puts it, "That's the important part."

Teague became the organization's first president. By 1990 the association had formed an agreement with

A milk bottle from the Route 66 Dairy, which operated in Springfield, Illinois, through the late 1950s, has found its way to the Route 66 Hall of Fame.

"The Beelers [owners of the Dixie Truckers Home] ended up building all those display cases for us. They've maintained them and improved the displays. We have never had to spend a cent for the maintenance or construction of the displays. The Dixie has always been very generous," says Tom Teague, caretaker of the Route 66 Hall of Fame and author of *Searching for 66.*

A Minnequa Water Bag "Cools by Evaporation," other goodies from the Cozy Dog, a limited edition print of artist Ken Turmel's Route 66 postmark collection, "Route 66 and More", and three examples of Chain of Rocks postcards at the Route 66 Hall of Fame.

Route 66 Hall of Fame caretaker, Tom Teague, visits with French tourists out traveling the Mother Road on a motorcycle tour.

the Beeler family, owners of the Dixie Truckers Home in McLean, a small, conspicuously midwestern town characterized by clean white houses, an old-fashioned town square beneath a giant water tower, and an early-1950s Chevrolet sedan laying upside-down in the weeds near what used to be the intersection of U.S. 66 and U.S. 136. The Dixie is reputed to be the oldest continuously operating truck stop on Route 66 and seemed to be the perfect high-traffic location for an informal, free museum waiting to surprise the unsuspecting traveler with cheerfully informative, simply presented nostalgia. The Route 66 Hall of Fame is literally in a hallway busy with truckers, diners, and 66 enthusiasts stopping intentionally or accidentally to learn about and remember the Mother Road.

Eight glass cases line the hallway filled with Route 66 memorabilia. While none of the items are of great physical size, virtually all are authentic artifacts. Some are obscure like the shield-embossed milk bottle from the Route 66 Dairy, a business that had a four-year run through the late 1950s in Springfield, Illinois. Some are well known like the jacket patches from Springfield's famous Cozy Dog eatery and a pipe from the grand organ at the Rialto Theater in Joliet. Others are downright famous such as the original sheet music for the song

"Route 66"—the only other example of which Teague has seen is owned by songwriter Bobby Troup's ex-wife, Cindy—and a rather odd, not-quite-authentic-looking highway marker sign that seems too small, thick, and heavy to have ever been on a post along the road.

"The sign that was actually used in [the title sequence of] the *Route 66* TV series is here," Teague explains. "It's a very, very heavy cast metal—a very solid sign with cut-glass reflectors. The way you can tell this is a special sign is that the cut glass reflectors on the sixes are not just clear glass, but rather, they have a greenish yellow cast to them. The reason for that is that the whole series was shot in black-and-white, and it made the sixes show up better on TV. As further documentation, on the back of the sign, there is a 'Universal Studios, Hollywood, California' property tag."

The Dixie Truckers Home is owned and operated by the fourth generation of its founding family, having been established in 1928 by J. P. Walters and his son-in-law, John Geske. Geske's daughter, C. J., married Chuck Beeler, and the Beelers are still involved, with the bulk of the business being handled by Chuck and C. J.'s son Mark. The Dixie burnt to the ground in 1965 but was pumping gas the next day.

"The Beelers ended up building all those display cases for us," Teague says. "They've maintained them and improved the displays. We have never had to spend a cent for the maintenance or construction of the displays. The Dixie has always been very generous. In addition, we have never had to pay to acquire a historic object."

The idea for a hall of fame per se came from Dr. Henry Maxfield of Mason City, Illinois, and was immediately

embraced by the association with Teague having his own reasons for liking the concept.

"The thing I liked best about it was that it would still be there when all the hoopla about 66 was gone. I figured all the fervor about 66 would fade someday, but we would still have the Hall of Fame."

OKLAHOMA
ROUTE 66 MUSEUM

It's the contention of Chicago's outstanding postcard collector, Jeff Meyer, that while the Route 66 nostalgia movement of the 1990s has been off to a great grassroots start, it will have to be turned over to professional history and tourism people for it to continue to grow.

Half-a-highway away in the western Oklahoma town of Clinton, Meyer's hopes seem to be met by the Oklahoma Historical Society in the form of the Oklahoma Route 66 Museum fronting on West Gary Boulevard—Clinton's proud segment of Route 66.

Oklahoma's leading-edge effort to preserve 66's history came to one of its lives as the Western Trails Museum in 1968 and was an example of the historical society's method of building a number of general Oklahoma history museums in various communities around the state. Through ensuing years, the society has found it wiser to build more specifically themed museums, and the Western Trails Museum began to evolve into a transportation museum. As the Route 66 nostalgia tide began to rise quickly, the Oklahoma Historical Society chose this site to go surfing—thus, the Oklahoma Route 66 Museum and its team of professionals. The museum's best year as the Western Trails Museum claimed approximately 8,000 visitors, but as the Oklahoma Route 66 Museum the facility had more than 27,000 paying visitors in 1998.

It's an Oklahoman, Cyrus Avery, who gets the lion's share of credit for bringing Route 66 into existence and creating its path, and Oklahoma is home to what today is the highway's premier museum.

The Oklahoma Route 66 Museum's tour begins with the building of the road and a display of some of the tools of the road-building trade.

The museum is roomy with space to grow and has a specific course for the visitor to walk through to experience Route 66 in order—from the introductory room to the road construction room, from the service station room with a 1928 International Harvester pickup truck to the 1950s diner room, from the motel sign room to the theater showing Route 66 documentary videos. Along the way are exhibits on the Great Depression, the trucking industry, tourist destinations, and a Volkswagen bus leaving the 1950s with a factory color scheme and coming through a partition into the 1960s with a Day-Glo psychedelic paint job illustrating the decade and culture of the great highway's death.

The Devil's Rope Museum in McLean, Texas, presents Route 66 to the visitor with nearly 100 percent original artifacts that offer fragments of what used to be found along the old highway. While the Oklahoma Route 66 Museum is not as packed with these original treasures, it tells a chronological story through photos and large pieces such as the visible gas pump and prewar truck in the service station exhibit and the 1939 Ford in front of the Capitol Motel sign that gives the scale to the sign's enormity.

The museum taken as a package has the historical presentation of a top-flight historical site and the slick marketing of a high-quality tourist trap.

"I've been lambasted for most of my career for being in favor of marketing heritage and getting people used to recognizing that if they want quality interpretation, they're going to have to pay for it," says former museum director John Hill. "Many places try to subsist on some kind of shoestring, and they never have enough money to do things, even on a minimal kind of basis, to really attract attention."

Professionally marketing history is what this museum does best, and the subsequent benefit to the visitor is the

The truth is that Route 66 was really built for truckers, and the Oklahoma Route 66 Museum has a small display of trucking industry–related photographs and company signs.

Many remember Route 66 as being their passage to new places, and the Oklahoma Route 66 Museum honors the tourist industry.

big, comfortable building housing large, complete scenes made to be walked through and not disconnectedly viewed through panes of glass. In the real world, Route 66's most engaging artifacts—the road itself, the railroad crossings, the cars, the 18-wheelers, the buildings, and the people—are all life-size, and the exhibits at the Oklahoma Route 66 Museum are life-size. They rekindle life-size memories for older people and give a life-size experience to younger people who would only have photograph-size experiences with 66 otherwise. It's called a museum, but Hill calls it an interpretive center where things are not viewed from afar but, rather, with inter-activity. Visitors can pump the handle on the visible gas pump and sit in the booths of the diner exhibit to

Below: Many would not have made it across America without the mechanics and gas station owners who fixed and fueled their vehicles. A 1928 International Harvester pickup has found a place to rest in surroundings it likes at the Oklahoma Route 66 Museum.

The Oklahoma Route 66 Museum honors the great American diner.

see what they were like, and even though the camera collection is behind glass, the barrier is set up deliberately to not interfere with visual experience.

The museum's gift shop sells the usual mix of modern souvenirs, and Hill's attitude toward making history accessible through marketing and profit extends to his attitude toward the items themselves.

"It does seem sometimes that if you stick a Route 66 shield on something, regardless of what it is, you'll be able to sell it," Hill says. "To me, it's an either/or, because if it's satisfying to the customer, I have no problem at all."

Hill says there are things the museum wouldn't carry, citing Route 66 toilet paper as an example of something to be avoided even if funny on some level. When the museum gets something custom made for sale, a 66 shield on the item is specifically requested because when items have been carried without the shield, they simply have not sold.

The museum invites visitors to write their memories in the museum's memory book, and Hill values these memories as being important input to the museum's understanding of the public's interest in the road.

"I gave a presentation, and I used a lot of the quotes from our memory stand where people had written about

A late-1930s Ford has found a place for the night under the neon at the Oklahoma Route 66 Museum.

when they were traveling Route 66 50 years ago or when they were traveling yesterday. There were three professors there, and they literally attacked me for talking about these memories because these memories were not talking about death on the highway or things like that. They were talking about the excitement of being on the road, and these professors said we didn't have anything about the death, the misery, and the hard times, and I asked them, 'Does that mean people can't legitimately talk about these good things?' People will choose what they want to find accord with, being politically correct is not what people want rammed down their throats anymore."

Route 66 seems to be a catalyst for memories important to the way America is perceived by its citizens and visitors.

"We're harkening back to what are sometimes called the kinder, gentler times," Hill says. "When I traveled as a child with my family on Route 66, my father did most of the driving, and when he'd get tired, he'd just pull off the side of the road and sleep a little bit. We'd all just sleep in the car. If you do something like that today, you might as well hang a sign on the car that says, 'I'm stupid. Kill me.' In those days, it wasn't anything at all to see a number of cars pulled off the side

of the road with people sleeping in them. That's not to say crimes never happened, but today no sane person would pull off the side of the road and go to sleep."

Former curator Heather Roulet, having been born in the post–Route 66 early 1970s, has a different take on Route 66's meaning to the museum's visitors.

"It's this fast pace of life we have," Roulet says. "People don't get to slow down for anything. If you have kids, you have a million different clubs and events to get them through, and some people just want to slow down and see what it was like [in a slower, simpler time]. Route 66 allows people to do that. There are a lot of people who still have businesses along Route 66, and they don't mind sitting down to talk for a while and tell the stories of the things that happened to them during the time they've been there. It's about being able to glimpse a slower pace of life and maybe being able to relax. When you turn on the news, you hardly ever hear anything good, and Route 66 is kind of a bright spot. The morals or ideas of an older generation are a bright spot they like to look to. They may not ever achieve those things, but in their minds, they would love to be able to."

Roulet considers people's happier memories of the highway to be important to this museum and the contents of people's private collections. "The people who collect gas station and diner memorabilia in particular [are remembering] vacations they took down Route 66," he says, "and they have really great memories of their vacations with their families."

As a young person involved professionally in Route 66, Roulet's interpretation of the Oklahoma Route 66 Museum and other collections is centered around recognizing anything that's about to disappear.

"A lot of people who experienced Route 66 are gone or getting very close to passing away, and people are wanting to record as much information as they can," Roulet says. "As a world and a people, we like to have information down. If we don't, we feel really bad because we didn't take that opportunity whether it's about our family histories or national history."

NATIONAL ROUTE 66 MUSEUM, ELK CITY, OKLAHOMA

Oklahoma seems especially proud of its history and has one of the most impressive state historical societies along Route 66. This love of what came before is also found at the city level, and the western Oklahoma municipality of Elk City is home to a city government-sponsored museum complex dating back to 1965 when land was set aside, historic buildings were moved in, new old-style buildings appeared, and Elk City's past came alive in a process continuing through the 1990s and into the twenty-first century. Authentic buildings include the first wooden house built in Elk City and the town's original school house with authentic period furnishings. Re-creations include the bank building, mercantile, barbershop, jewelry store, funeral home, and soon-to-be introduced drugstore with an old-fashioned soda fountain operational on special occasions. Nearly all of these were fashioned in Elk City's founding period of 1901.

While the National Route 66 Museum wasn't conceived as part of the museum complex until 1989 and didn't open its doors until 1997, Route 66 has played a part in the complex's plans for decades.

"The Route 66 theme has been woven into it from the beginning," says City Manager Guy Hilton. "The road was really the main thing that made our economy vital. We are about halfway between Amarillo and Oklahoma City and always had more motel rooms than most towns. Right now, we have something like 1,000 motel rooms in Elk City, and that's pretty unusual for our size of town. We've always been a stop-off point between those cities on either Route 66 or I-40. We have today about 36 restaurants here. So, from the very beginning of Route 66, [serving the traveler] has been

Still photographs cannot capture the grandeur and beauty of the mural map of the Mother Road at the National Route 66 Museum in Elk City, Oklahoma. The map was painted on a curving wall by Fort Worth, Texas, muralist Stylle Read and shows every town that was ever on Route 66.

a big part of Elk City, and that is the reason it's always been threaded through the museum. The [rest of the museum complex] is about what a home would look like at the turn of the century, and then, there's another section that shows all different displays of early–Elk City memorabilia. The upstairs is a rodeo museum dedicated to the Butler Brothers who are rodeo stock producers who live here, and they've been [stock producers] since the 1930s or 1940s."

While the Oklahoma Route 66 Museum in Clinton takes a focused look at Oklahoma's role in 66 and 66's role in Oklahoma, the National Route 66 Museum peruses Route 66 as a nationwide entity with vignettes representing each of Route 66's eight states.

While dedicated to the past, the National Route 66 Museum boasts some high-technology. Hanging above a visitor's head are Plexiglas umbrellas containing sound equipment, and as the visitor walks under one of the umbrellas, voices from the past begin to tell their tales. Taken from authentic accounts of Route 66 travel, the National Tape and Disc Corporation has marketed *Route 66—A 60-Minute Audio Magazine* of these 66 travel memories. These tales accompany the visitor through the museum without the visitor having to carry earphones, push buttons, or read long passages from placards that distract from the experience of hearing the memories while looking at Route 66's recently rediscovered relics. Accounts include a man's memories of his honeymoon vacation to California with his new bride in the 1940s and his laments at traveling not being as interesting on today's interstates. An Oklahoma farm wife shares her experiences during the Dust Bowl's beginnings and her struggle to ready her family for the journey to California. An Oklahoma

It's tourist season at the National Route 66 Museum, and as tourists move about the museum, they trip sensors that trigger recorded readings of authentic Route 66 travel memories. These stories range from the Oklahoma farm wife readying her family for a desperate trek to California to the gentle-voiced man remembering his honeymoon in the 1940s when he and his new bride headed for fun in California. He says traveling isn't as much fun on the super-slab and laments the passing of a far more interesting roadside.

farmer shares his memories of having to stop and get a job in a diner in New Mexico on his way to California, which led to his owning the diner for life.

Dr. L. V. and Pat Baker have been key figures in Elk City's museum commission since 1965, and Pat Baker served as the commission's first chairwoman.

"We all grew up along Route 66," says Pat Baker, "so, a lot of us on the museum commission got thinking about the road and thought it would be nice to save it. Michael Wallis' book came out about a year later, and between all these things, it got the excitement rolling. We all grabbed hold and decided we needed to do something about it because it's such a vital part of the nation's history."

The Bakers and the rest of the museum commission are responsible for the museum's themes and displays.

The trip through the museum begins outdoors, whether the museum is open or not, with a representation of 66's heyday built and painted into the side of the museum building.

"On the outside of the building, we depicted businesses that people would have noticed along Route 66," Baker explains. "We tried to stay away from depicting actual businesses so that people would apply the images to the businesses that were next to them or that they remember stopping at. We made a little drive-through lane so people could stop their cars and take pictures of their car in front of a Route 66 theme. We tried to make photo opportunities."

Indoors, the museum's floor is dominated by a large, U-shaped, mural-covered wall. On the inner side of the curving wall is a symbolic diner scene with silhouettes of happy eaters in the windows and a real 1955 Mercury parked in front with a food-filled tray hanging on the driver's windowsill, drive-up restaurant-style. On the outer

Fuel up at the National Route 66 Museum in Elk City, Oklahoma.

side of the wall is an impressive map of Route 66's trek across America. These large works of art were painted by muralist Stylle Read of Fort Worth, Texas.

"He's just a wonderfully talented young man," praises Baker, "and we were able to get him to be pretty much our live-in artist for close to a year. He stayed and did all the murals, and the map is to scale and shows *every* town that was ever on Route 66 so people can look up the towns they remember as they go through the museum."

Guy Hilton and Pat Baker both make sure to mention their enjoyment of watching the visitors and listening to their reactions to the displays.

"It's been heartwarming to see young families—people who are bringing their children and letting them soak up the energy and tales of Route 66," Baker tells. "All the superhighways are so busy now, and it's wonderful to see people getting off the interstates and getting back into the small towns to walk around in the park and come into something that makes them feel at home. [I think they've been missing that], and I think they're beginning to come back and pick it up again."

They called it devil's rope.

DEVIL'S ROPE MUSEUM, MCLEAN, TEXAS

They don't consider themselves archeologists, but barbed wire collectors can identify a few inches of it to a period, a manufacturer, a use, and a location—each of which has a story of its own. A post hole digger, a pair of pliers, or a fence-stretching tool found buried in the sand near a forgotten fence on an abandoned ranch can tell a barbed wire collector exactly when that fence was built and maybe who had the contract to supply the materials. Whether they brag about it or not, these are the textbook characteristics of archeologists, and the results of their "digging" have been seen at the Devil's Rope Museum in McLean, Texas, since 1991.

McLean has all the ills afflicting many Route 66 towns. Though still home to a large natural gas plant, a turbine engine repair shop, and a centrally located feed store, the traffic is gone; the farming isn't what it used to be; and the dying local businesses have left empty commercial space to rot. A big building dominates one of the cross streets between the east- and westbound lanes of 66—a building big enough to have housed a brassier factory with 100 employees beginning in the 1940s. It now houses the Devil's Rope Museum and submuseum dedicated to Route 66, which according to museum volunteer Delbert Trew, boasts one of the largest percentages of authentic artifacts of any Route 66 museum; no reproductions here. Other than a few items on loan, all the Route 66 pieces belong to the museum.

Volunteer labor from an informal group of barbed-wired enthusiasts made this museum what it is—a maze of hand-built displays showing a myriad of barbed and razor wire types, barbed wire manufacturing tools, fence stretchers, post hole diggers, augers, and historic cattle brands. Around every bend are the tools that, in their day, meant unending toil, but today mean understanding the past struggles that made a frontier manageable.

Within a few decades, Route 66 swept across the frontier right behind the barbed wire, following its path along railroad easements, and a Route 66 museum swept in behind the wire again at the Devil's Rope Museum.

"Sixty-six is a very recent part of history that [younger people] can actually go out and find," says Delbert Trew. "It's almost impossible to find a Colt six-gun like we used in 1880, but you can reach back into the Route 66 days, and depending on how much

A tangle of neon motel signs hangs from the joists of the Devil's Rope Museum in McLean, Texas. A sign invites visitors to throw the switch and watch the signs going into their buzzing, flashing, clattering, eye-grabbing rituals.

money you have in your pocket, you can buy an old reflector or more modern sign."

The Route 66 display is dominated by the super-sized metal snake that sat ready to strike in front of the Regal Reptile Ranch in Allanreed, Texas, for decades—it's lumpy contours and crude welding making clear its true purpose to lure tourists into a zany, unintentionally campy rattlesnake museum. Glass cabinets are filled with small toys from roadside businesses, motel ashtrays, and gas station memorabilia. Photo displays in the re-creation of a life-size diner tell the story of Groom, Texas. Over it all hang neon motel signs, and when the placard that invites visitors to throw the switch is obeyed, the signs light, the internal mechanisms start to hum and cycle through their rattling paces, and the flashing white bulbs trimming the signs begin their complicated dance. A row of Burma Shave signs impart their wisdom below a hand-painted map of Route 66's path through Texas.

Route 66 has gained heavy interest among people clearly too young to remember the road's heyday firsthand, and the Devil's Rope Museum has its share of young visitors who seem to be looking for something hard to define.

"I think [the younger people] are tired of plastic," Trew continues. "I think they're tired of TV. I think they're tired of the freeway and the fast lane, and they're saying there's got to be more to life than this; I really do. One thing we're finding is that old hippies are really interested, and it may be the first time they were really interested in anything, but they're coming back."

Approximately 75 percent of the Devil's Rope Museum gift shop is devoted to Route 66 memorabilia, and this proportion is reflected in sales volume. The shop has the usual fare of modern Route 66 souvenirs with an exceptionally well-organized, library-like display of its

The Devil's Rope Museum maps 66's path across the Texas Panhandle.

Even a very small 66 town can have a rich history, and the Devil's Rope Museum houses a collection of photos chronicling the tornado damage once suffered by Groom, Texas.

All people like to eat, and all Route 66 museums like diner displays. Here we see the life-size diner display at the Devil's Rope Museum.

books and videos. Unique to this gift shop, of course, are the samples of historic and identifiable barbed wire mounted on finished wood frames, making for a very masculine gift for the gentleman in a lady visitor's life.

Trew takes collecting seriously and seems to like what he senses in the minds of many of the museum's gift shop customers.

"If you buy an inflatable soda bottle that has nothing to do with Route 66 except for the two numbers printed on it, well that's kind of frivolous," he says, "but if you come to the museum and buy a book or a pin that you can wear, I don't consider that frivolous. There's nothing frivolous about barbed wired. You *have* to be interested in barbed wire if you're going to collect it. There is a bit of a frivolous fad to Route 66, but I think that's fast coming to an end."

Trew says collecting is part of American culture because up to only a few decades ago, every girl had a hope chest, which was "essentially a get-married kit"

in Trew's words, and this collection was taken very seriously because this was the kit to start life. Trew says any kind of collecting is no longer that serious. As with collectors of some other generationally important items, the collectors of barbed wire are getting older, and the most desirable barbed wire collectibles are getting expensive—thus, making the addition of the Route 66 display to the Devil's Rope Museum a carefully timed adjustment. Trew thinks it's an important function of the museum that as visitors come to see the 66 displays, they discover other things along the way.

"Route 66 was not only the path of flight, it was also the path to discovery because when you get out and start trying to find Route 66, you start finding places like this, Red River War battle sites, and you find prisoner-of-war camps," he says. "There are several categories

of visitor. You have the people coming back who actually traveled 66 in times of trauma or flight or catastrophe, and they're coming back to see if it was actually as tough as they remember. We are also seeing a group of younger people coming out here looking for the missing links—the missing parts. They want to find things no one else has found yet."

CALIFORNIA
ROUTE 66 MUSEUM

"Ah, the 1950s," many nostalgists wax. It was a time of endless prosperity, peace, and suburban bliss. Route 66 was at its busiest and most popular, making for prosperous roadside businesses and culture—right?

Had the 1950s really been that comfortable, the California Route 66 Museum probably would not exist.

Delbert and Ruth Trew, devoted barbed wire enthusiasts and caretakers of the Devil's Rope Museum.

Victorville's poured concrete Halstead Building was originally built in 1918 to demonstrate the product of a local cement plant.

While small- to medium-size by Route 66 museum standards, the California Route 66 Museum boasts one of the finest photograph collections on public display along 66.

Victorville, California, nestled in a little valley against blissful relief of the Mojave River, was the gateway to the hot, harsh Mojave Desert to the eastbound 66 traveler and, for many of them, the overnight stop after climbing over the slow, steep, treacherous, hot-in-the-summer, cold-in-the-winter Cajon Pass. In the early 1950s, Victorville's 3,000 inhabitants made their livings at cement plants and mines, large electric and telephone facilities, and a variety of roadside businesses. Many of Victorville's downtown buildings dated to the 1900 to 1920 period with newer buildings steadily appearing over the years to the south and west, following 66 toward the Cajon Pass.

Well before the death of 66, three things happened to Victorville: A housing tract was built on Victorville's southern outskirts in 1953; an up-to-date, neon-covered shopping center with a post office, supermarket, hardware store, and drugstore was built across 66 from the new housing tract in 1955; and a new alignment of 66 bypassed all of Victorville in 1956.

To Victorville, the 1950s meant its original downtown was in serious, though slowly developing trouble. In the early 1960s, Victorville incorporated as a city, and most of the car dealers moved to a new, farther south edge of town along 66. In the 1970s, the civic center and county facilities moved to another even farther south edge of town along the former 66. In the 1980s, a giant, modern mall opened miles farther south along the path of the long-dead 66—all of it leaving Victorville's original downtown devastated.

In the 1990s, the Old Town Victorville Property Owners Association decided they'd had enough. The business face of the organization became the California Route 66 Museum, the essence of which originated in a

The California Route 66 Museum's superior photo collection includes this aerial comparison of Victorville's pre- and postwar eras. The 1938 photo (left) was taken to assess flood damage, and the 1961 photo (right) was taken to track improvement progress to the 1955 bypass of Victorville by Route 66-91. The two photos show the growth of Victorville to the south that began draining its downtown of life.

conversation between several property owners in the late summer of 1995. In November of that year, the museum's doors opened for business, making for what has to be one of the quickest museum births ever. The museum moved into the history-oozing Halstead Building, which fronts Route 66's surface street incarnation as D Street, one block from where 66 turned to follow Seventh Street. The Halstead Building was built in 1918 of poured concrete to demonstrate a local cement company's product, and one of its first tenants was the First National Bank, which fell victim to the Great Depression in 1931.

The museum's collection is a conglomeration of donated and loaned items that are loosely organized, but the facility has earned bragging rights for housing some of the best historic photographs on display in any Route 66 museum. Panoramic photos—some nearly 4 feet in length—taken in the 1920s, 1930s, and 1940s containing long, recognizable stretches of 66 through Victorville dominate the displays. One panoramic taken in 1917 of the Southwest-Portland cement plant on the north side of Victorville shows more than a half-mile of National Old Trails Highway, which became Route 66 nine years later. The museum's own block is represented in three different photos and panoramics taken between

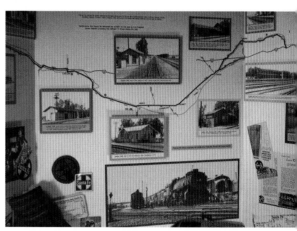

The Western Railroad Museum's contribution to the California Route 66 Museums is this map illustrating the Mother Road's relationship to the rails. In the Southwest the wagon roads followed the water, the railroads followed the wagon roads and the water, and Route 66 followed the railroads.

Among the California Route 66 Museum's authentic artifacts is this hand-painted map of the Mojave Desert's highways from circa 1960. The map was a decoration in Riley B's bar and grille next to the Halstead Building until the by-then abandoned tavern burnt to the ground in 1996. The map miraculously survived.

1900 and 1947 and in a number of color postcards taken circa 1960. Two aerial photos of Victorville—one taken in 1938 to assess flood damage and one taken in 1961 to gauge progress of adding on-ramps and off-ramps to the 1955 bypass—document the southward expansion of Victorville during the 1950s that began draining the old downtown of its life.

Well to the south of Victorville was a man of slight eccentricities. Miles Mehan was an ex-carnival worker who set up a roadside stop in the 1950s consisting of wacky displays, like posts with colored bottles attached called "bottle trees," a strange little miniature golf course with clubs weathered to the point of disintegration, and a stand of decorative hubcaps called "Hubbie." Everywhere one turned were Mehan's poems painted on wooden signs—poems dedicated to the memories of Mehan's local friends and fellow carnival workers like Dead Eye Toby, Fast Draw Eddie, and Stink Foot Fred and dedicated to local events like the night Victorville's Green Spot Cafe burned down on the curbs of Route 66. High above it all was the goddess of Route 66 roadside campiness keeping some travelers entertained and others wondering. Known affectionately to the locals as the Hula Girl, from her image came the other name for Mehan's Half-Acre—Hulaville. The Hula Girl started her life as a

Hulaville's namesake, the famous Hula Girl, who welcomed 66 travelers to the Mojave Desert for decades is safely stored at the California Route 66 Museum and destined to be displayed in the museum's future facility. Without museums' efforts to preserve some of Route 66's odder artifacts, they would be destined for the county dump and lost forever.

Authentic items from Miles Mehan's wacky roadside open-air museum, Mehan's Half-Acre, aka, Hulaville, on display at the California Route 66 Museum.

Re-created in miniature by California Route 66 Museum volunteer Steve Anderson, Hulaville lives again. Anderson says he "got good with his hands" having been afflicted with polio in his feet as a child, and he says the museum's display of miniatures will continue to grow and represent more of Route 66. Hulaville proprietor and poet, Miles Mehan, can be seen represented in blue jeans and red suspenders smiling at the curious and amused forever in the miniature display. The museum keeps alive the fading personalities along America's Main Street.

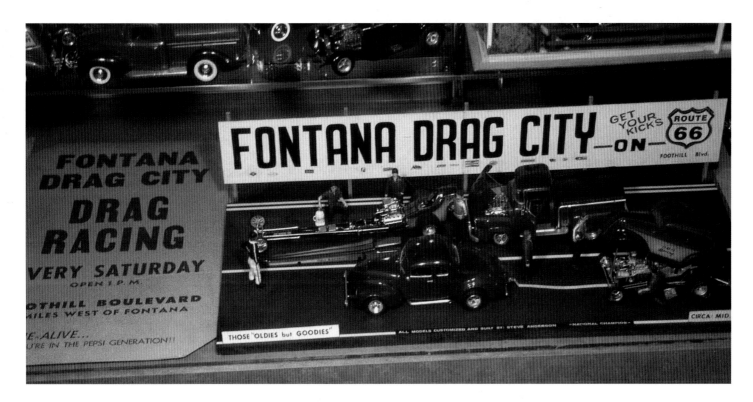

FONTANA DRAG CITY DRAG RACING VERY SATURDAY OPEN 1 P.M. OTHILL BOULEVARD MILES WEST OF FONTANA E-ALIVE... U'RE IN THE PEPSI GENERATION!!

FONTANA DRAG CITY —ON— GET YOUR KICKS ROUTE 66 FOOTHILL Blvd.

THOSE "OLDIES but GOODIES"   ALL MODELS CUSTOMIZED AND BUILT BY: STEVE ANDERSON   *NATIONAL CHAMPS*   CIRCA: MID

sign atop a restaurant in Los Angeles, and upon demolition of the restaurant, Mehan rescued her, and she thanked him by keeping watch over Hulaville for approximately 40 years. Strolling the grounds for decades was Mehan, selling little books of his poems.

The California Route 66 Museum collected Hulaville upon Mehan's death in 1998 at age 100. The poems, the bottle trees, the signs, and the all-important Hula Girl are all displayed once again to the 66 traveler in the California Route 66 Museum. Without that museum, these items surely would have wound up in the county dump, illustrating the importance of museums in the struggle to preserve the common things that disappear so quickly upon changing times.

In addition to boasting high-quality photographs, this petite museum also claims some of the best miniature re-creations displayed about and along Route 66. The creations of Steve Anderson, these roadside images tell silent but complete stories. The old man stuck by the side of the road with a steaming Ford Model T has painted "I'll give it a kick!" on a sign below a Route 66 marker near him. Racing fan and former employee of

drag-racing pioneer "Big Daddy" Don Garlits, Anderson has re-created the Fontana Drag City racing strip that fronted Route 66 in Fontana, California, through off-the-line racing's 1950s and 1960s golden era. Taking the cake as Anderson's most ambitious achievement for the museum is his stunning replica of Hulaville complete with miniatures of Mehan, the Hula Girl, and all of Mehan's signs, with Anderson having even replicated Mehan's handwriting in the painted style of the poem signs. When one's eye is brought down to this miniature Hulaville's ground level, the scene is eerily realistic with all objects to scale, all displays showing desert weathering, and Mehan watching visitors watch him with a satisfied grin on his face.

Subsisting on the gift shop, some donations, and a little grant money, the California Route 66 Museum is taking Victorville, the Mojave Desert, and Route 66 into the twenty-first century and pulling the urban sprawl back to Old Town Victorville by reminding the local population and traveling visitors why this town grew from its humble roots as a river crossing into a once-thriving piece of highway-side small-town America.

Steve Anderson's re-creation of the Fontana Drag City racing strip at the California Route 66 Museum. The strip faced Route 66 in the form of Foothill Boulevard. in Fontana through drag racing's golden age—the 1950s and 1960s. The sign at right is an authentic phone pole placard from 1963.

CHAPTER 5

Selling 66

Author Michael Wallis frequently says Route 66 has always been a commercial enterprise, and there's nothing wrong or unusual about this historical artifact being marketed and sold. From its early promotions such as the Bunyon Derby through later exhibitions such as the Will Rogers Highway procession, Route 66 was perpetually sold—much to the delight of the highway's roadside business owners.

With passing time, the highway fell from favor, was bypassed by the interstate system, and descended into decay. In the 1990s, a nostalgic and hurried America wanted to slow down and rediscover its traveling roots, and like the early days of selling Route 66, the nostalgic dollars spent along the highway are rebuilding its culture.

Some places selling the highway are themselves historic. Eisler Brothers Old Riverton Store in Riverton, Kansas, brings back the friendly neighborhood grocery store.

Tee Pee Curios of Tucumcari, New Mexico, continues its tradition of giving the westbound travelers their first dose of southwestern goodies.

Meteor City near Winslow, Arizona, has had a long history of giving rest and mementos to weary travelers in an especially remote region.

The Hackberry General Store of Hackberry, Arizona, continues the heritage of its previous owner and focuses on its own special stretch of the highway.

Other locations have more recent histories but still bring Route 66 to the traveling public.

The Old Route 66 Emporium in Staunton, Illinois, guides the traveler over two fascinating alignments of

A familiar sight for hundreds of miles on Route 66. The signs counted the miles to Arizona's famous Jack Rabbit Trading Post.

Author Michael Wallis asserts Route 66 has always been commercial, and the proof can be seen to this day along the eastern Arizona highway.

the highway and honors the truckers who made their livings on the route.

The Big Texan Gift Shop has sold Texas souvenirs to Amarillo visitors for decades but has recently realized the importance of Route 66 to its early days.

The Route 66 Place-Twisters and *Route 66 Magazine*'s gift shop are recent arrivals on the scene but have put Williams, Arizona, back on the map. Angel Delgadillo was a barber into his 60s, but an inspiration and some memories converted his retired barbershop into a Route 66 collector's paradise.

All have in common that their stimulation of Route 66's roadside business climate reflects a tradition in keeping with the history of selling the road.

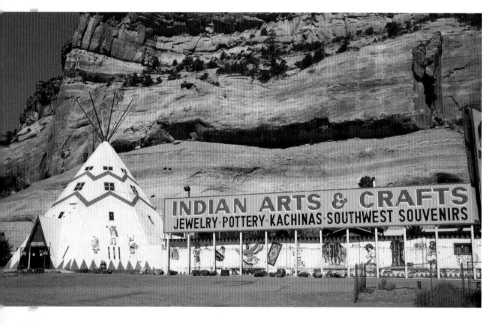

OLD ROUTE 66 EMPORIUM

As with most young people at the time, Route 66 didn't mean much to Rich Henry while he was witnessing the highway's heyday. For him, the thoroughfare was just part of his father's job and his own first couple of jobs. Henry didn't know that decades later, he would be providing Route 66 nostalgists and travelers with their mementos and availing people of his knowledge about the road when he later became the proprietor of the Old Route 66 Emporium in Staunton, Illinois.

Rich and Linda Henry were both born in 1947 and both grew up on America's Main Street.

"I grew up in northern St. Louis, and in the '60s, I worked at a Mobil gas station on Bypass 66 [now the path of Interstate 270]," Rich Henry tells. "I also worked at a trucking company on the east end of the Chain of Rocks Bridge, and I crossed that bridge every day to go to work. We would have to pull-start some of the trucks to get them started in the winter, and we would pull them right on Bypass 66. We would have to wait for the traffic to die down so we could pull them down the highway. When I was working at the Mobil station, people would use their Mobil credit card, and I would have to write down their license plate numbers. I never understood why I was seeing all these people from Arizona and California. I used to wonder why they were so far east. I used to watch all these trucking lines go by. I didn't realize the importance of it, but I was looking at Route 66. I wish I'd had a camera and taken pictures of the intersections full of the cars and trucks of the time."

Bypass Route 66 took drivers around congested, urban St. Louis and sent them across the Chain of Rocks Bridge into Illinois. With the coming of the interstate era; Bypass 66 itself was bypassed and forgotten, but as the 1990s unfolded, Route 66 nostalgia spread from its beginnings in Arizona and Illinois. Awakening to the realization that an alignment of Route 66 ran along the east side of a piece of commercial property they owned, the Henrys opened the Old Route 66 Emporium in 1993 in the town of Staunton amid the clean, flat, fertile ground of Illinois.

Rich Henry inherited his father's love of trucking and is still proudly a part-time trucker, making the familiar runs between central Illinois and central Missouri along Route 66.

The trucking theme is strong at the Emporium. Campbell's 66 Express tractor-trailers were a familiar

Rich and Linda Henry of the Old Route 66 Emporium in Staunton grew up on Route 66.

sight to midwesterners during the heyday with the trucks adorned with the company's cartoon logo, Snortin' Norton the camel, running his heart out above his motto "Humpin' to please." Two of these trailers have found a home at the Emporium, and a variety of Campbell's memorabilia dresses the interior of the store.

"That attachment to Campbell's is from having grown up with trucking in my blood, and trucking and Route 66 go together like a husband and wife," Henry says. "The trailer is a great attention-getter, and the people who mess with old cars for a hobby are attracted to the old trucking notion. Campbell's is a great icon to people from the Midwest, having started the same year as 66. Everyone growing up remembers the trucks with the camel on the side. It was so different from any other truck line at the time."

Rich's roots as a gas station attendant make themselves evident with a number of vintage gas pumps and Phillips 66 items on display.

While handling the usual lines of modern Route 66 souvenirs, the added bonus of gathering them at the Old Route 66 Emporium comes from the personalities and experiences of Rich and Linda Henry.

"We're right on Route 66, and we're Route 66 people. My wife lived on it, and in my case, I rode it with

my dad. We understand it, and we care about the history of the road and preserving it. We take the time to talk with people. I'll be surrounded by all this work I should be doing, and someone will come into the store, and we'll start talking. Next thing you know, an hour-and-a-half has gone by, and we're still talking. That is something you can't get at all Route 66 gifts shops: people who were actually there. The big, modern truck stops will add up your merchandise and tell you it's a buck and a quarter. It's not their

Rich Henry grew up traveling 66 with his trucker father. The Old Route 66 Emporium takes special notice of truckers in their collectibles on display and for sale.

job to attempt any conversation. Here, people are looking for stories and information, and here, they get it. The most a truck stop cashier will say is 'have a nice day.' Here, our average conversation lasts about 45 minutes."

After helping an Aurora, Illinois, school girl with her class project by sending her some information and items to show, Henry received a letter of appreciation from the girl that mirrors his family's attitude toward their customers.

"It was a big thank you letter, and that was more gratifying than selling a $1,000 worth of merchandise."

EISLER BROTHERS OLD RIVERTON STORE

No one knows for sure, but the timing's right. Leo and Lora Williams built their store fronting Route 66 in 1925 after a gas station and store on the next lot to the east was destroyed by a tornado in 1923. This little store in Riverton, Kansas, filled the void when someone needed something in the 1920s. Seven decades later, the store fills a more abstract need.

"When things start to disappear, those that are left become a little more sacred, and you begin to preserve what you're about to lose," says Scott Nelson, manager of the Williams' little store, known since Nelson's Aunt Isabelle and Uncle Joe bought it in 1973 as Eisler Brothers Old Riverton Store.

With the exception of missing the tall glass-bowl gas pumps that appear in old photos of the site, the building has changed little since the 1920s. Red brick on the outside and a cheerful yellow on the inside highlight a well-preserved pressed-metal ceiling that screams of the Jazz Age. At dusk, the renewed green-and-red neon bars that border the store's canopy begin to glow as the original ones did through the 1940s and 1950s. The smells of garlic, peppers, cheese, and smoked meats and the sights of decades-old grocery store counters, shelving, and equipment greet the walk-in visitor.

Roughly two-thirds of the building was devoted to the store originally with the other third having been the Williams' small but comfortable living quarters. The store has expanded into the living quarters, which now houses the gift shop devoted completely to Route 66 collectibles

Eisler Brothers Old Riverton Store, facing 66 since 1925, might owe its existence to a tornado. The building once had gas pumps in front, and the neon has been restored to its 1940s glory.

The sights and smells of a 1920s neighborhood/highwayside grocery store. The smell of gasoline is gone from the Old Riverton Store, but the peppery aroma of an old-fashioned deli greets the customer. The Jazz Age–pressed metal ceiling is always a hit with the "old stuff" seekers who travel 66.

of the modern varieties—T-shirts, mugs, key chains, antenna balls—but it wasn't a scheme that brought success to the gift shop.

"I'm all for planning, but some things just happen, and this is something that just happened," Nelson tells. "A guy from Waynesville, Missouri, came in and had little Route 66 buttons that we bought. Then, a friend of mine saw some T-shirts, and we ordered a few. We found out people liked this stuff, and it kind of snowballed."

Route 66 enthusiasts are looking for the atmosphere of the road. Eisler Brothers is a chance to obtain souvenirs in the authentic atmosphere of the nearly extinct neighborhood grocery store and receive that atmosphere and more.

"They're seeing a part of America you don't see when you go to the popular destinations. There may be 10,000 people traveling Route 66 between Chicago and L.A., but they're so spread apart, it's like you have the whole road to yourself. It's not like standing in line to ride the latest roller coaster for that two-minute thrill."

Scott Nelson is the welcoming presence who runs the Old Riverton Store with some help from his father, Forrest.

Nelson says roughly 10 percent of his business is generated by the Route 66 gift shop with the number climbing to about 30 percent in peak tourist season, and as all notice along 66 a significant chunk of Eisler Brothers' gift shop business stems from foreigners.

The Old Riverton Store was founded by Leo and Lora Williams in the 1920s, and today's Route 66 gift shop is in the Williams' former living quarters.

"They're seeing life in a nostalgic way when things weren't so complicated, and another thing [the foreigners] have said is that they're seeing the real America. As the old saying goes, when you travel on the train, you see America in its shirt sleeves. You see the good and the bad."

All Route 66–oriented gift shops are doing their best to bring their businesses and neighborhoods back up from the dust after the slump. They all deserve credit, but Eisler Brothers is the recipient of a wonderful accident—being America's favorite kind of traditional grocery store and facing America's favorite highway during a very nostalgic time.

Modern collectibles can still have a connection with history when gathered at a historic place like the Old Riverton Store.

THE BIG TEXAN GIFT SHOP

He's in all the books, videos, and photo collections, and he induces a Texas-sized reaction from Route 66 enthusiasts who finally see him in person. Barreling along the Interstate 40 super-slab through the Texas Panhandle's flat, southern-plains nontopography can make a driver glad to see civilization in the city of Amarillo. Well within the realm of the city, there he stands high in the sky with a classic Southwest cowboy hat, a six-shooter on his hip, and a proud, welcoming smile—the Big Texan.

He didn't always face an interstate, though. He began his life on the Mother Road—Amarillo Boulevard—some distance from his present location.

The Big Texan has been greeting Amarillo passers-through since 1960.

Some argue that the Big Texan is not relevant to Route 66 today because it faces Interstate 40, but the establishment started its life at this location on Amarillo Boulevard, Route 66's original eastern approach to Amarillo. The big Texan's historic sign is still with us because the establishment moved to I-40 and survived.

Route 66 gained momentum, the merchandise of the gift shop began to fill this new need.

While modern and nonhistoric, the gift shop still has a unique atmosphere that lends a significance to the souvenirs purchased there—memories of a place like no other. Route 66 items of the modern varieties are everywhere with the white shield plastered on just about everything. The shop's method of displaying its reproduced signs across heavy open beams gives a sense of distance to all the states represented.

The western diamondback is a big rattlesnake, and they run good and thick in this corner of Texas. All through the gift shop are diamondback items unique to the region—heads with fierce fangs exposed, rattle-covered tails, and entire snakes coiled ready to strike are there in taxidermy. Allanreed, Texas, 70 miles to the east

"People want so much to be a part of [Route 66] that they're willing to spend dollars on it that they would have spent on other types of souvenirs. The dollars spent on 66 are going to be what preserves it."—Frank Jordan, owner, Big Texan Gift Shop

He's been serving Texas-style steaks, ribs, and barbecued everything to travelers and locals since 1960, and in the years since his move to I-40 in the early-1970s, he's challenged big appetites from around the world to eat a 72-ounce steak with all the fixin's in less than an hour with the payoff being the meal at no charge. The dozens of winners sign their names in a big book at the bar along with their comments, ranging from "That was easy" to "Ughhh!"

The Big Texan retains its traditions of good food, lots of noise, and musicians roaming the tables. As interest in

The gift shop is under separate ownership from the rest of the Big Texan. Frank Jordan bought the gift shop in the late 1990s.

"The road is old and needs dollars to keep it up, and it's fine [that history is being marketed]," says Jordan. "People want so much to be a part of it that they're willing to spend dollars on it that they would have spent on other types of souvenirs. The dollars spent on 66 are going to be what preserves it."

TEE PEE CURIOS, TUCUMCARI, NEW MEXICO

Even on today's Interstate 40, it can be a five- or six-hour drive from Amarillo, Texas, to Albuquerque, New Mexico, and in the days of crowded, two-lane Route 66, this time was easily double from what it is today. From the plains of the Texas Panhandle to the Sandia Peak of Albuquerque, Route 66 glided over long, red sand flatlands and wound around red cliff mesas, rising and falling much to the frustration of truckers. There were scorching desert temperatures in the

While not as historic as some, the Big Texan still provides Route 66 goodies in an atmosphere like no other.

George greets visitors at the Big Texan Gift Shop and poses for photos in spite of his relatives being on the Big Texan menu.

of Amarillo, was home for many years to one of Route 66's famous landmarks—the Regal Reptile Ranch—where motorists could get their fill of rattlesnake mementos, and the Big Texan Gift Shop gives today's Route 66 searchers a chance to relive the kinds of merchandise handled by the venerable Allanreed institution.

Watching the gift shop is George, a 5 1/2-foot western diamondback with a big set of rattles and a pleasant disposition. He relaxes in his spacious terrarium watching customers and posing for photos. When he wants attention, his rattles can be heard clear outside the shop door many feet away. He seems content while surrounded by his brethren's heads and tails, seeming to prefer his cushy home to dodging tires on Route 66. Some of his friends are on the Big Texas restaurant menu: "Genuine diamondback rattlesnake by the piece. We want to warn you there is very little meat and lots of bones. Any complaints will get you a live one."

"It's OK to make money because that's what Route 66 was all about, but if you want to keep Route 66 alive, you need to buy your collectibles at the genuine, historic, small businesses in smaller towns."—Mike Callens, Tee Pee Curios, Tucumcari, New Mexico

summer and icy wind and snow through the winter. Little New Mexico towns served the traveler's needs through the harsh region—Glenrio, San Jon, Clines Corners, Quervo, Moriarty, and the medium-sized Santa Rosa.

Those who've driven this stretch at night have seen the shining jewel in the distance looking like Oz to weary eyes, hungry stomachs, and empty gas tanks. Leading drivers to the sanctuary for miles in advance are those famous signs—"Tucumcari Tonight!"—and fronting the highway for many years has been the ornate, charming, and genuine Tee Pee Curios, which started its life in the early 1940s as a gas station owned by Lelands and Iva Lee Haynes where the signs read, "Lelands' Gulf-Curios-Groceries," according to present Tee Pee owner, Mike Callens.

"When 66 was two lanes, there were gas pumps out front," Callens tells. "When they enlarged the highway, they lost the gas pumps, and it became strictly a curio shop. I would venture to say this change took place in the late 1950s or so."

In the mid-1960s, the Hayneses sold to a Prado family who only owned the location for a short time before selling to Callens' aunt and uncle, Jean and Earlene Kleverweiden. While many parts of Route 66 were being bypassed by the late 1960s, times were still good for Tucumcari.

"Jean and Earlene took it over just in time for the heyday, and through the time they had it, it was called Jean's Tee Pee. They really made money in this business."

Competition was stiff in the curio business through the good times of the 1960s and 1970s, and the Kleverweidens hired Indians to weave and dance in front of their store to catch the eye of passing traffic.

Tucumcari was bypassed in 1981, and by 1985, the Kleverweidens were looking to sell. Living in the Los Angeles area, a laid-off Mike Callens was looking to get back to his Tucumcari roots.

Tee Pee Curios screams of the good times of Route 66, sitting only one block and across the street from the famous Blue Swallow Motel. The building's teepee

The items may be mass-produced, but gift shops like Tee Pee Curios provide a memory to go along with them.

theme, clean white surfaces, and iron bull's head sculpture on the front make it one of the first icons of the Southwest seen by the westbound traveler.

Modern Route 66 souvenirs are everywhere along with Tucumcari gifts such as mugs, hats, and buckles. Callens reports that items with the Tucumcari name on them are among his best-sellers because "'Tucumcari Tonight!' is a great image."

Route 66 enthusiasts out to collect memories through souvenirs will enjoy Tucumcari-specific collectibles more than if they had to remember where they got them.

As with Arizona's Meteor City and Angel Delgadillo's Route 66 Gift Shop, the Route 66 traveler will receive the advantage of being able to obtain souvenirs *and* memories at a historic location with a strong and genuine connection to the Mother Road. There may also be the satisfaction of doing right by the small business owners who gave Route 66 its living, breathing roadside culture.

"When you look at Route 66 passing through Tucumcari, you see the town is all motels," Callens says. "Tucumcari was here to serve the tourists and travelers passing through. All the motels are still here, but with the increased speed limits, and the chain restaurants and motels going up at the off-ramps, the independent motels are dying. When the chain stores go in at the off-ramps, it's a cancer to small business because travelers can spend the night, eat, and get all they need without ever venturing into the town. By buying gifts or spending the night on the old main streets of these old towns, you're helping to keep Route 66 alive as opposed to those [corporate-owned] businesses just out to make some money. It's okay to make money because that's what Route 66 was all about, but if you want to keep Route 66 alive, you need to buy your souvenirs at the genuine, historic, small businesses in smaller towns."

While it may run in phases, Callens seems to believe the public's curiosity and desire to slow down and remember will keep the Tee Pee around for some time.

"Hey, we ain't throwing in the towel," he says. "We ain't going anywhere. We came here to get out of the rat race, and we're here for the long haul. We enjoy talking with all the people who come through the door. To me, the slow pace is part of the payoff. A lot of the people who come through there are living life too fast, and [life on two-lane Route 66] is a great way to not be part of that."

THE ROUTE 66 PLACE AND TWISTERS, WILLIAMS, ARIZONA

"Ah, the '50s . . ." It's a phrase heard over and over along Route 66. While some historic-minded enthusiasts bristle at the *Happy Days* version of the 1950s dominating all pop-imagery of the decade, most

Tee Pee Curios from the drawing pen of Bob Waldmire.

TUCUMCARI, NEW MEXICO (Alt. 4,087 FT.) — HOME OF THE TEE PEE CURIO STORE — "DAMN FINE STUFF". BUILT IN THE EARLY 1940's WHEN RT. 66 WAS ONLY TWO LANES, THE TEE PEE STARTED OUT SELLING GULF GAS & GROCERIES, WITH A SIDELINE OF CURIOS. AS 66 GREW, THE STORE LOST ITS GAS PUMPS TO THE WIDENING ROAD. IN ITS HEYDAY IT WAS BUT ONE OF MANY CURIO STORES BIDDING FOR BUSINESS FROM THE THOUSANDS OF CARS THAT WERE PASSING BY DAILY. BUT IN 1981 TUCUMCARI WAS BYPASSED BY I-40 & IT SPELLED THE END OF AN ERA. NOW THE TEE PEE IS KNOWN FOR BEING THE LAST OF THE OLD RT. 66 CURIO SHOPS LEFT NOT ONLY IN TUCUMCARI, BUT IN EASTERN NEW MEXICO. P.O. BOX 734, TUCUMCARI, N.M. 88401

OLD ROUTE 66 scenes! © 11-95. R. Waldmire 43

For a couple of hundred miles in each direction, giant billboards extoll the virtues of "Tucumcari Tonight!" to this day, making the remote city and Tee Pee Curios a natural for both unhurried nostalgists and hurried modern travelers.

samplings of Route 66 travelers will reflect the positive sentiment. A healthy dose of 1950s good times can be had in Williams, Arizona, at the Route 66 Place gift shop and its adjoining soda fountain, Twisters.

The Topock-through-Seligman section of Route 66 crossing western Arizona is one of the most popular stretches in all the highway's length, and it's home to the annual Route 66 Fun Run. East of Seligman, a traveler is treated to another 18 miles of two-lane pleasantness nearly to Ash Fork before being forced onto Interstate 40 for another 20 miles for the fairly steep climb to Williams. Along this section of I-40, the old alignment of 66 can be seen crossing the interstate in long, sweeping curves that surely forced trucks to a crawl and made for slippery conditions through a snowy winter. Many people were ready to stop after this climb or the long ride from the East through the prairies of the eastern half of the state, and Williams has always been alive with motels, eateries, gas stations, and neon.

The Gateway to the Grand Canyon is the town's registered trademark, and it claims thousands of tourists a year to see the natural wonder. Williams has always had a railroad presence, and the town is home to the Grand Canyon Railroad where tourists can ride to the canyon on a train pulled by an early-twentieth-century steam engine in the summer or a 1950s-vintage streamlined diesel engine through the winter.

Williams has the distinction of being the last piece of Route 66 bypassed by the interstate system. On October 13, 1984, the I-40 bypass of Route 66 opened with a ceremony that marked the end of an era, and it was no longer necessary to drive Route 66 at any point between Chicago and Los Angeles.

Dave Pouquette is a Williams native who remembers the 1950s well, having been born in the early 1940s. He retired from the Coconino County Sheriff's Department in 1985 after 20 years as a deputy, holding the office of undersheriff at the time of his retirement. He

Dave Pouquette poses in front of the double business, the Route 66 Place and Twisters in Williams, Arizona, where Grand Canyon tourists often get their first exposure to Route 66. Says Pouquette, "People remember the things of the '50s so fondly now because they were unique to those good times. Travelers remember those things, and today they're trying to find them again. I think in a lot of cases younger people are trying to find the good times their parents had. There's a lot more to traveling across America than a white line and 75 miles per hour."

went into the real estate business in Williams, and by mid-1995 he bought a building and exercised an idea he'd had for some time.

"It was opened with a soda fountain in mind," Pouquette tells. "When I was growing up, there were always two soda fountains in town. Both of them were in drugstores, and after the last one went out, I always wanted to open one. One thing lead to another, and first came the fountain, then came the '50s theme, then came the old cars and Route 66. It was a natural because we're right here on Route 66."

The Route 66 Place-Twisters combo is a modern Mecca to 1950s nostalgia kitsch—from the 1954 Chevrolet and pink 1956 Ford Crown Victoria parked outside to the sweeping chrome with black-and-white tiles of Twisters. The sales floor of the Route 66 Place is dominated by modern Route 66 collectibles with a wide selection of western clothing as well. While not housed in a historic site or bestowing historical accuracy, Route 66 souvenirs gathered at the Route 66 Place can still be enjoyed much the way authentic souvenirs from the past were when they were first gathered.

"The family vacation was an icon of the '50s," Pouquette says. "The destinations were really of little importance to the kids in the car. They were out to see the reptile gardens, the teepee-shaped motels, the bright neon, or other entertaining things. The business people built these eye-catchers to try to get travelers to stop, and it worked. People remember these things so fondly now because they were unique to those good times, and travelers today are trying to find and collect those things again. I think the reason they gather them is to have a piece of the memories that they lived. A guy who hitchhiked across America many years ago will look at that 66 sign in his den and remember those days. It's unbelievable what those memories mean to people."

Other travelers discover Williams and the Route 66 Place by accident.

"We get lots and lots of folks who are just on their way to the Grand Canyon. They come here looking for the Grand Canyon, discover Route 66, and get pretty excited about it. They hear the old '50s music we play, see the merchandise we're displaying, and start remembering back when they were kids. We had a guy walk in here recently, and he said, 'My god! This is better than the Sears tool department!' I felt like I'd had the ultimate compliment."

Somewhat more than a neo-'50s shell, Twisters can supply an authentic cherry phosphate, a tart beverage nearly extinct since the 1960s, to a new generation of nostalgists looking for the flavors of the past.

Twisters also serves up cuisine unseen in many years.

"We still serve cherry phosphates," Pouquette says. "That's something you haven't been able to get since the late-'60s or so. We also serve the flavored Cokes that were so popular years ago—chocolate, cherry, vanilla—and we serve what soda fountains used to call a suicide Coke with all the flavors in it at once. What passes for a milkshake today is nothing like what soda fountains used to serve. Today, they squirt muck out of the machine and call it a shake. We serve the true malts, which are surprisingly hard to get today."

Pouquette has turned to the mythic side of the 1950s because he is not in the museum business and seems to place his focus on what Route 66 travelers are out to experience and collect on their vacations.

"People remember the *things* of the '50s so fondly now because they were unique to those good times. Travelers remember those things, and today, they're trying to find those things again. I think in a lot of cases, younger people are trying to find the good times their parents had. There's a lot more to traveling across America than a white line and 75 miles per hour."

ROUTE 66 MAGAZINE, PUBLISHING HOUSE, AND GIFT SHOP

Route 66 Magazine began with the winter 1993 issue. Why?

"Because there was a need," says publisher Paul Taylor. "There was a resurgence of Route 66 at that time. It was coming back to life, and there was a need for a publication to disseminate information on an international basis to people who were interested in the highway."

Within two years, the magazine moved from a remote location to the heart of its namesake.

"We were publishing the magazine out of Laughlin, Nevada, and there were a number of businessmen up here who thought the magazine would help the economy of Williams. We considered it for about a year, and we finally accepted. We found a store and refurbished it, and business has been going really well. A year after we moved in, we received the 1997 Arizona Main Street Award from the governor's office for being the fastest growing business in the state at the time and were recognized as a new business that had contributed significantly to the economy."

Publications can be thought of as miniature books. They can be bound, shelved, and collected just as books are, and the quarterly arrival of *Route 66 Magazine* can build a collection of information and images produced by some of Route 66's greatest authorities. Dan Harlow, Jerry McClanahan, Jim Ross, and many more take readers through the history, culture, and sights of Route 66 past and present. Between books on 66 and updated information found in *Route 66 Magazine*, a potential traveler, enthusiast, or historian can collect an education.

Inspired by the magazine, readers and travelers may wish to visit the publisher's offices and gift shop in Williams. Housed in one corner of a historic 66-facing

The pleasantly cluttered and unashamedly kitschy interior of the Route 66 Place.

Paul and Sandi Taylor publish *Route 66 Magazine* from Williams, Arizona. Says Paul, "Williams is a piece of tangible Route 66 that's still here with the stores lined up along Route 66 as they always were. Some come to touch Route 66, and some just discover Route 66 while they're here."

Dating to 1909, *Route 66 Magazine*'s home was originally Babbit Brothers department store. The building's future includes a museum, expanded gift shop, 200-seat theater dedicated to historical documentaries, and a radio station playing music from the middle of America's glorious twentieth century.

building dating to 1909, history can still be felt in the modernized interior of the gift shop, and souvenirs—no matter how modern—can still carry a historic significance if purchased in Taylor's shop.

"One unique thing is that Williams was the last community to be bypassed by the interstate system," Taylor says. "Williams is a piece of tangible Route 66 that's still here with the stores lined up along Route 66 as they always were. Some come to touch Route 66, and some just discover Route 66 while they're here."

Also unique to the high, mountainous, pine-shrouded Williams is its main attraction—the Grand Canyon. Always full of sightseers, the town provides by nature the tourism other Route 66 gift shops usually need to create for themselves. The main highway may have been moved out of town, but the Grand Canyon hasn't budged an inch and still fills the town with tourists seeking or discovering Route 66.

One of the few Route 66 gift shops able to experience ongoing evolution, the store is expanding throughout the building, and plans for the first decade of the twenty-first century include a 200-seat theater, an enlarged gift shop, and a radio station playing music from the 1940s and 1950s, with the broadcast studios in the window and using as much period equipment as possible.

Selling 66 has kept the highway alive in Williams, and Taylor thinks this in itself is a continuation of an American tradition.

"History is marketed from grade school on. History is documented through school books, which are marketed to the schools," he says. "History is marketed all the time from different companies. There are reproductions of things like classic cars and airplanes from The Franklin Mint. It's how we get a hands-on feel for history. There's nothing wrong with marketing history. We're buying history by buying a book on classic cars. It's an opportunity. You should enjoy history. I wish I had realized this when I was in school and being forced to study history."

DELGADILLO'S ROUTE 66 GIFT SHOP, SELIGMAN ARIZONA

The country is lonely for miles and miles on either side of the little western Arizona town of Seligman. To the west are the prairie expanses of the Aubrey Valley, and to the east are curves and grades that negotiate the rising topography through Ash Fork and up the mountains to Williams. Once a thriving cattle town with a railroad yard and breathing roadside, Seligman was a small but potent success story with glowing businesses and a massive railroad station.

The cattle business slowed. The railroad yard and roundhouse were removed. Then, Interstate 40 bypassed Seligman by at least a mile with exits into the town being long and somewhat confusing.

Angel Delgadillo is the son of a barber and speaks with the gentle lilt and deliberate kindness of a classic Latin gentleman in his 70s. His words best describe the beginnings of the "original" Route 66 Gift Shop he started in Seligman in the late 1980s and the reasons his name is known around the world by collectors looking to find their treasures at the origin of the modern Route 66 nostalgia movement.

"I experience it every day. How? When that person walks through that door grinning from ear to ear, and he says in his mind, 'I have found him! I have found the place where it all started!' I relive that every day," Delgadillo says. "They are so happy to have found Seligman, Arizona. It's like they're looking for the tire prints."

The tire prints lead to a barbershop. Delgadillo took over where his father left off. The senior Delgadillo's

barbershop was on the original highway through Seligman right against the railroad tracks and next to the train station. Angel's shop was on the modern alignment of Route 66 through the heart of Seligman. The shop occupied a small corner of the building with room enough for one comfortable barber chair, and the rest of the building was devoted to a popular pool hall. With

The publishing offices of *Route 66 Magazine* double as a gift shop serving Mother Road enthusiasts and Grand Canyon tourists.

Finding one's way down Route 66 at the *Route 66 Magazine* gift shop.

had that feeling again. The world stopped, but this time the lonesomeness lasted for years. You could walk out into the highway, look both ways, and nothing came. There was no traffic. This town died. The world could not wait for the superhighways to be opened, and by the early 1980s, the traveling public got their taste of it. They drove from point A to point B, and they never saw anything. They started coming in here and saying, 'When I was a boy . . . When I was a girl . . .' I thought, my gosh, if the economy of this town is ever going to come back, maybe the state will make the highway historic.

"At chamber of commerce meetings, I would try to talk about Route 66, and no one wanted to listen to me. I finally said, 'Route 66 is our next project, and if you're not going to go with my idea, I'll go at it myself.' I called a meeting February 18, 1987, at the Grand Canyon Caverns, and 15 people showed up. I presided, and we

It could be argued that the entire Route 66 nostalgia movement began at Angel Delgadillo's barber shop, and collectibles gathered here may have the distinction to the collector of having been acquired at the center of it all.

passing time, rails, and highways, the shop became home base to the founding of a movement.

"I remember when our late president, John Fitzgerald Kennedy, was assassinated, the world stopped," Delgadillo says. "The world went into mourning. One part of that I remember so well was that I was walking down to visit my brother, and there was a tumbleweed blowing from the north to the south because the wind blows that way here. It was such a lonesome feeling. When we were bypassed September 22, 1978, we

"I experience it every day. How? When that person walks through that door grinning from ear to ear, and he says in his mind, 'I have found him! I have found the place where it all started!' I relive that every day. They are so happy to have found Seligman, Arizona. It's like they're looking for the tire prints."—Angel Delgadillo from his shop

John and Kerry Pritchard with their labor of love, the Hackberry General Store. It began its life as the South Side Grocery and much later became Bob Waldmire's Old Route 66 Visitor's Center before progressing into the Pritchards' hands. "We don't want to sell Route 66 from Chicago to L.A.," says John. "We want to sell Route 66 from Seligman to Kingman. This is our stretch of road. Route 66 is great, but I can't tell you what it's like in Chicago or Kansas. I want to tell people what it was like right through here."

gelled. We called ourselves the Historic Route 66 Association of Arizona, and the rest is history."

This small Arizona town in the middle of nowhere is constantly filled with old cars and tourists from all over the world. All are there to see where today's Route 66 phenomenon began, to photograph a quaint old town filled with preserved roadside culture, to have a burger at the Snow Cap Drive-In owned by Angel's humorous brother, Juan, and to collect their fill at the Route 66 Gift Shop which, in addition to today's souvenirs, has on display small but moving artifacts. These include hats worn by genuine Seligman cowboys through the decades, early-twentieth-century photos on the walls of the elder Delgadillo's original barbershop, newspaper clippings, and street scenes from Seligman's past. Bursting with photos are large albums on the pool tables, and visitors are invited to take a long look at photos from the past and present of Route 66.

Like author Michael Wallis, Angel Delgadillo is a collector of people too. On the walls of his barbershop are the business cards of thousands of visitors from over the years. Angel smiles broadly and makes a visitor feel important when he places the visitor's card on the wall, saying, "This is your place in my shop." Between the lines, one can tell this also means a place in Angel's heart and in the hollowed ground of a shrine to a movement.

HACKBERRY GENERAL STORE,
HACKBERRY, ARIZONA

A native of Illinois, Bob Waldmire is a favorite among Route 66 devotees. His artistic maps and postcards are seen in all the gift shops along the road, and his images educate and delight roadies all over the world. In the early 1990s, Waldmire relocated to the

tiny town of Hackberry, Arizona, where he established the Route 66 Visitors Center to rescue an old building and bring an ecological bent to Route 66. Passing time took Waldmire back to Illinois to become involved again with his father's famous Route 66 establishment, the Cozy Dog.

During his time in Hackberry, Waldmire made the location famous as thousands of Route 66 Fun Run attendees, journalists, and photographers met him and came to understand his purpose. Since selling the location to John and Kerry Pritchard, the building has returned to its roots as a general store.

Route 66 runs blade-straight northeast out of Kingman through a valley so flat that a driver can see

Showing its age also means showing its history, and the Hackberry General Store gives the collector a feel for the grittiness of rural Arizona in the 1930s.

every inch of 19 miles of blacktop. The road goes over a little rise and curves more directly east, and Hackberry is nestled in a little valley about 25 miles out of Kingman. Route 66 used to run on the east side of the railroad tracks but was later relocated to the west side, most likely to eliminate curves and bottleneck underpasses that negotiated the tracks. This move took 66 out of the town of Hackberry itself.

"The building was a 22-acre homestead established in the early 1930s, and it was always a service station and store," John Pritchard explains. "When they brought the highway up to where it is now

instead of through town, there were three grocery stores up here. They were all in a row, [but because of the way the road curves] they were called the East Side Grocery, North Side Grocery, and South Side Grocery. This was the South Side Grocery."

The Pritchards discovered Waldmire and his store while attending the 1998 Route 66 Fun Run. With time, the Washington State residents made a return trip, got to watch the store for a month, and made a deal with Waldmire, promising to never tear down the building. They intend to keep the store and their merchandise very connected with their section of Route 66.

"We don't want to sell Route 66 from Chicago to L.A. We want to sell Route 66 from Seligman to Kingman. This is our stretch of road. Route 66 is great, but I can't tell you what it's like in Chicago or Kansas. I want to tell people what it was like right through here. I want to tell people about the mining and the history here."

Hats, T-shirts, mugs, and Kerry's hand-crafted jewelry all reflect the Hackberry theme, making them unique to this one shop. Uniqueness is sought specifically by some Route 66 souvenir collectors, and the uniqueness of the Pritchards' merchandise will most likely be what keeps their shop alive against the competition of many large chain stores only a half-hour away in Kingman.

John's pride and joy is his 1957 Chevrolet Corvette. The *Route 66* television show permanently

Route 66 and the Indian culture of rural Arizona find their ways onto Kerry Pritchard's hand-crafted jewelry.

stamped the Corvette on Route 66 in the minds of many tourists, and the image of the Pritchards' red-and-white example finds its way onto most of their unique gifts, as do images of the building. It's a wooden structure of early-1930s vintage that still screams of its days as an Esso gas station that closed in 1974, according to Pritchard. The best Route 66 gift shops are those that offer an atmosphere for the collector to remember years after buying the object, and the Hackberry General Store offers a musty, dusty, splintery tone that typifies much of the Route 66 experience through the Desert Southwest. This image on the souvenirs keeps that experience alive for tourists who are trying to find it for the first time or old-timers who want to feel it again.

"We've gone back and tried to stock things you don't find at every store. We try to sell things that say 'Hackberry' on them. We sell all the Route 66 and Harley-Davidson stuff that you can find anywhere, but 75 percent of our sales come from merchandise that says 'Hackberry' or has a picture of our store and Corvette on it."

The store has become a long-term project devoted to making the tourist feel at home in the remote atmosphere of a little Arizona town, and Pritchard reports a growing amount of visitors from Kingman looking for some unique recreation close to home and a chance to experience the welcoming tone of a mom-and-pop roadside store once so common along Route 66 and other highways.

"It's fun and exciting for us even though the place usually only pays for itself through the summer months. I love seeing the people who come in here, and the joy the things we have bring to people. It brings back good times and memories. If they walk out of there with just a 50-cent candy bar, we're satisfied because they've had a fulfilling experience. We try to make them feel at home and show them we're glad they're here."

CHAPTER 6

Route 66 Collectors

They are as different from each other as night and day, but they all have Route 66 in common. Their collections are gatherings of recognizable authentic artifacts, forgotten fragments, art, and ephemera. From beautiful photos to splintered, rusted relics; from things meant to be collected to piles of meaningful rubble; from beautifully crafted works of art to rusty tin cans made special by the road; from officially acknowledged artifacts to self-styled collectibles made by the collectors.

The collections reflect the individual characters of the collectors, and the focus of each collection was usually arrived at through a series of wonderful accidents. In another arena a Buick collector would collect all things Buick, but Route 66 spanned over 2,000 miles and seven decades. The collectors were limited by a number of factors: There was no official definition of a Route 66 collection as there

would be with the Buick collection. There was no centralized place to view the objects and begin gathering. There were matters of differing budgets that caused some collectors to begin making their own collectibles, and for those who started before Route 66 was "cool," there wasn't even a way to look up what one would find interesting.

The resulting self-defining world of Route 66 collectibles took shape, making for individual collections containing radically different items. Route 66 has made for a collecting world like no other.

Michael Wallis' collection surrounds him with authentic road markers and the rarest of one-of-a-kind artifacts, but his prized possession is a tiny piece of a broken statue and the little story it tells.

Jeff Meyer started collecting before it was cool, and while his collection boasts authentic markers and

Collector and roadologist Jeff Meyer of suburban Chicago is surrounded by the objects that trigger winter dreams of his next road trip.

113

Author Michael Wallis showing that one of his favorite Route 66 collectibles is also one of the simplest: "A little thing I found was a tiny Madonna face outside a graveyard in New Mexico. I found it while visiting the dead, and it really means a lot to me."

pieces of historic locations, his collection of 7,000 post-cards from Route 66 has accidentally become a great tool of archeology.

Becky Ransom discovered that the school she was teaching in was on Route 66, and she used her collec-tion of Mother Road trinkets to excite her students into wanting to study twentieth-century history.

Steve Rider lives many miles from Route 66, but the collection in his Route 66 Garage brings the road much closer.

Individualistic, hard-to-define, and somewhat wild and wandering in their focus, these collectors and their collections are, in a word, eclectic.

MICHAEL WALLIS

Route 66 had many beginnings—from Cyrus Avery in the 1920s to the rail-and-wagon roads that set its path, from the desperate launch of westward migra-tion by Great Depression–era refugees to the surge of postwar prosperity. Even after Route 66 slowly decayed in usefulness and lay fallow through most of the 1970s and 1980s, a new beginning was in the works. A small number of articles and books about 66 were quietly

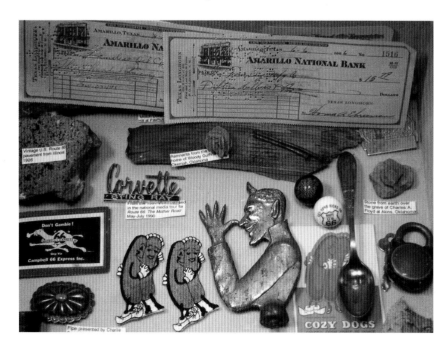

This box of goodies in the Michael Wallis collection features a snakeskin from the Allanreed, Texas, Regal Reptile Ranch; patches from the Cozy Dog eatery of Springfield, Illinois, where the corndog was perfected; and checks from a Glen Rio, New Mexico, business written against an Amarillo, Texas, bank account.

Michael Wallis proves that a meaningful Route 66 collection can be largely made up of fragments. Wallis gathered these pieces during his 1990 book tour.

published during the 1980s, and the Nickelodeon television network broadcast reruns of the *Route 66* television series in the mid-1980s, most likely as just a neat old TV show than a piece of historic consciousness.

Then came 1990, and Michael Wallis' book, *Route 66—The Mother Road*, hit the bookstores and became the work that woke the sleeping giant and made Wallis one of the fathers of the tremendous Route 66 revival.

Wallis' collection, which includes authentic highway markers, Phillips 66 gas station signs, and numerous items from roadside businesses, is large and overwhelming. In a big, cluttered room on the top floor of Wallis' Tulsa, Oklahoma, home, the scattered remnants directly reflect the scattered nature of Route 66's artifacts after the fall of its popularity and usefulness—tiles and glass bricks from the Coral Court Motel, snake skins from the Alanreed, Texas, Regal Reptile Ranch, and a double-edged ax head reputedly having belonged to writer D. H. Lawrence while living in Santa Fe, New Mexico.

Diversity is a key word to describe the Wallis collection. Manufactured trinkets from today's selling of nostalgia reside near one-of-a-kind artifacts that have value beyond Route 66 such as the teacher's podium from a 100-year-old school in El Reno, Oklahoma.

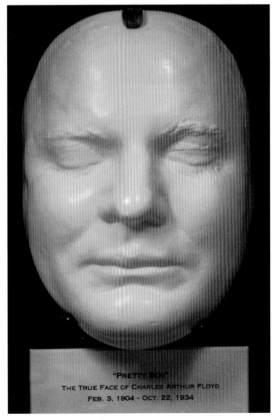

"PRETTY BOY"
THE TRUE FACE OF CHARLES ARTHUR FLOYD
FEB. 3, 1904 – OCT. 22, 1934

Pretty Boy, the Life and Times of Charles Arthur Floyd is Michael Wallis' biography of the infamous bank robber who expressed a preference for Route 66 as a speedy escape route. His activities included committing his first armed robbery in St. Louis and being captured once in Tulsa—both Route 66 towns. Upon being gunned down by law enforcement in Ohio in 1934, a plaster cast was made of the robber's face, and this authentic example resides in the Michael Wallis collection.

The Club Cafe was a fixture of Route 66 through Santa Rosa, New Mexico, and this rare cap graces the home of Michael Wallis.

After publication of *Route 66—The Mother Road*, Wallis became recipient of hundreds of gifts from Route 66's past and present, and his book became the recipient of a Pulitzer Prize nomination. While still retaining several file cabinets full of the highway's history and documents, Wallis has donated the bulk of his document collection to organizations such as the Missouri Historical Society.

Author of 10 books during the 1990s, Wallis' books include *Pretty Boy, the Life and Times of Charles Arthur Floyd*—a biography of the notorious midwestern armed robber in which Wallis details Floyd's preference for Route 66 as a high-speed path of escape with high and low points in his criminal career occurring in St. Louis and Tulsa. When finally killed by police in Ohio in 1934, a plaster cast of Floyd's face was made to immortalize the face of a killer. Wallis' collection includes one of Floyd's authentic death masks. Floyd's face is peaceful and softly rounded with the expression of a sleeping child, which conceals his reality as a robber and killer.

This stark reality of Route 66's dark side is in direct contradiction to Wallis' warm feelings toward the little charms from the same road. Two of the first things Wallis mentioned when asked about his collection were his "lucky" coyote fang found near Clinton, Oklahoma.

"It's a nice little totem that keeps me from harm's way," says Wallis in the low, warm voice familiar to Route 66 enthusiasts. "Another little thing I found was a tiny Madonna face outside a graveyard in New Mexico. I found it while visiting the dead, and it really means a lot to me."

While authentic pieces of the past mean the most to Wallis, he is famous for insisting that Route 66 has always been a place of commercial enterprise, and those commercial efforts are what have given nostalgists their most treasured collectibles.

"[Today's manufactured collectibles] can be thought of as echoes of Route 66," he says. "I don't have a problem with the white shield being slapped onto things because people know the difference, but of course, I have a problem with anyone who lies about the authenticity of artifacts that aren't real. I still buy the kitschy, modern trinkets, too, because it appeals to me and gives me a chance to be a kid again."

Route 66—The Mother Road has in itself become a collectible. Today's Route 66 devotees are known to carry this and other books on their Route 66 vacations and seek out the personalities profiled in the book for autographs, illustrating the self-styled collectibles created by enthusiasts in a world of rare, expensive authenticity and common, manufactured trifles.

Born in the 1940s, Wallis is a proud baby-boomer, and while his generation has been criticized for frivolous values, Wallis maintains that his generational connection has helped shape his value of history, which includes Route 66.

"I'm a little bit hippie, I'm a little bit rebel, I have a little poetry in my soul, and I've thankfully retained some of the idealism that inspired me and spurred me on during those turbulent 1960s," Wallis tells. "I think there are a lot of us still around today—more than people might think.

"I'm out on Route 66 all the time, and every time I turn over a rock, out comes a new character. I'm always meeting new people. The best collectibles of all are my people. They're wonderful! Some of them, I've never even known their names, but I collect those memories, and I treasure those memories. Those stories are there in my heart forever, and those are the best things I've ever collected."

JEFF MEYER

A classic baby-boomer, Chicago native Jeff Meyer now remembers the height of Route 66, its song, its TV show, and its usefulness, but like many, Meyer forgot about the road only to rediscover it at its lowest point. The old highway's roadside held powerful images for Meyer, and his effort to gather those images has lead to a collection of nearly 7,000 postcards. The collection represents a usefulness that few collections can boast— a tool of commercial archeology.

Meyer married his wife, Laura, in 1984, and the couple decided to honeymoon in California but changed their plans due to the crowds and traffic descending on the Olympic Games in Los Angeles. They decided a road trip was in order and quickly discovered quiet, interesting, lonely Route 66 while passing through Springfield, Illinois. The Meyers immediately embraced the highway, and calling themselves "roadologists," began taking yearly road trips. In 1988, the roadologists made it all the way to California and met many people along the way who would become extremely important to the later Route 66 nostalgia movement.

Jeff and Laura Meyer, artist and Cozy Dog heir Bob Waldmire, and historian and author Tom Teague held a

"[Today's manufactured collectibles] can be thought of as echoes of Route 66," Michael Wallis tells. "I don't have a problem with the white shield being slapped onto things because people know the difference, but, of course, I have a problem with anyone who lies about the authenticity of artifacts that aren't real. I still buy the kitschy, modern trinkets, too, because it appeals to me and gives me a chance to be a kid again."

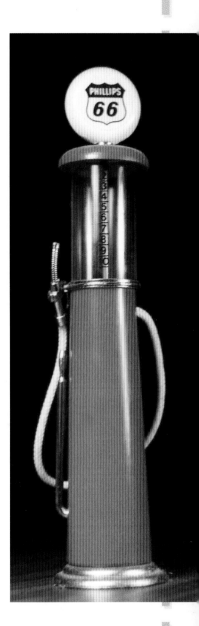

meeting in Waldmire's '60s-retro school bus in 1989 that created the Historic Route 66 Association of Illinois.

Meyer is rather modest—not calling himself a historian or archeologist—but Meyer's collection has grown into a source of historical verification and education. During Route 66's heyday, photography was a luxury on which most business owners didn't waste time or money, and they naturally didn't realize the daily grind of making their livings would be fascinating to later generations. In many cases, postcards are the only existing photos of roadside establishments, and Meyer's collection is a resource for the historian trying to verify when a building was remodeled, when the highway was widened, which part of a building was built first, when the gas pumps were added or taken away, or who the owners were at a given time.

"For example, the Munger Moss Motel in Lebanon, Missouri, started out with little garages between the buildings," Meyer explains. "They eventually closed in each of the garages and wound up with one big motel."

For Meyer, the enjoyment of his collection holds a much simpler but important pleasure, saying that it brightens cold Chicago winter days to open a box and dream of the old days of the road, his past travels, and his future destinations. His collection is arranged by state and stored in shoe boxes that stretch 10 feet when set end-to-end, and the cards are a virtual tour of the Mother Road, encompassing businesses, tourist traps, natural wonders, and road scenes. For the Route 66 novice, Meyer's collection would be a journey through time and one of the quickest, easiest educations on the road's look, atmosphere, and geography. The youngster

may find the texture and mood of other times, and the oldster may see sights he never thought he'd see again.

"Here comes a cliche, but people are trying to find a simpler time in America—a time when America wasn't rush, rush, rush or, at least, perceived that way," says Meyer. "They're trying to perceive a time when America wasn't in a hurry—a hurry to go nowhere. Once the soldiers got back from the war, went back to work, and got their two-week vacations, they started to head out on the road. Places like the Blue Swallow Motel were in their heyday. The Club Cafe in Santa Rosa was in full swing, as were all the [individually owned] ma-and-pa-type restaurants and motels."

Meyer thinks people look to their postcard collections to see individuality in the neon signs, architecture, and come-ons—no two alike and all vying for maximum attention.

"There's still a sense of adventure on 66 because you never know what you're going to find around the next curve. The whole idea today is to slow down and smell the roses. People look to the postcards to remember a golden era when Americans traveled along the U.S. highway system, pre-interstate, before America became generic, and we wound up with the Holiday Inns, the Denny's, and the McDonald's. One McDonald's in Chicago is the same as one in Santa Rosa or Tucumcari."

Do the curious see in Meyer's postcards the myth or the reality of Route 66?

"Collecting the myth rather than the reality is a good thing in a way. It was 'bloody 66,' and we should be aware of that historically, but I think the myth will serve the people still out there along the highway better than reality by getting travelers back out there and back into the small towns—back into the diners and back into the motels and hotels along the route."

Meyer and his wife divorced in the 1990s, and Lynn Bagdon of suburban Chicago has become Meyer's traveling companion. Bagdon has for a number of years made her own Route 66 collectibles based around her little friend, Luscious Lulu—a sexy rag doll with fishnet stockings and a come-hither glance who travels with Bagdon posing for photos throughout the length of Route 66. Authentic artifacts from the reality of Route 66 may not always be easily found or affordable, but Bagdon has photos of Luscious Lulu in front of and inside famous roadside establishments and with Route 66 personalities.

Bagdon also has a penchant for seeking out classic Phillips 66 gas stations. Bagdon has, thus, created her own collectibles for no more than the price of film and processing, and her collection is unique and without a hint of being generic or manufactured.

Meyer thinks Route 66 preservation efforts will become more professionally led in the twenty-first century after getting off to a great grassroots start in the 1990s, and no doubt, his collection will become a valuable resource for those professional historians trying to untangle the archeological web of Route 66. With these efforts, Meyer believes the Route 66 movement will be perpetuated and gain more respect than a mere fad would ever have.

"If [66] were a fad, it would be gone already."

BECKY RANSOM

Becky Ransom was born in Jackson, Wyoming, in the early 1960s, but it wasn't until the late 1990s that she realized the importance of the venerable and historic Lincoln Highway to her native state. As Ransom used her interest in Route 66 to teach U.S. history to her sixth-grade classes in Amarillo, Texas, she discovered for herself and imparted to her students tangible histories that live and breathe beyond the abstract names, dates, and places that quietly molder in the pages of typical history textbooks. All historical elements were, in their times, as real and tangible as today's things and events, but for a child, history can seem dim and unreal until a catalyst comes along that brings history to life in concrete "3D." Ransom's collection of Route 66 trinkets and memorabilia became tangible, touchable history for her students.

College took Ransom to her first 66 town—Springfield, Missouri—and after graduating in 1985, her first teaching job took her to Amarillo where 66 had occupied Sixth Street and Amarillo Boulevard at different times. Her Mother Road discovery process began in 1988 when she took a part-time job at the Panhandle's famous Big Texan Gift Shop for extra income through the school's summer months and vacations. In spite of being on the banks of Interstate 40 by the early 1970s, the Big Texan and its renowned cowboy-in-the-sky sign had originated in 1960 on the curbs of Amarillo Boulevard and, today, is still celebrated as one of the great Route 66 landmarks. As the 1990s, commenced,

Jeff Meyer's postcard collection stretching out more than 10 feet. Numbering more than 7,000, Meyer's postcards represent 2,400 miles and nine decades counting the cards from the pre-Route 66 1910s.

Ransom began noticing some new arrivals in the Big Texan's display cases.

"In 1992, I noticed we were getting a little more Route 66 merchandise in the gift shop," Ransom recalls. "I met Michael Wallis in 1993, and we had a book signing for him at the store around that time. I became fascinated with the whole thing. It was the history that grabbed me. I've always loved history, and this was history I could actually experience. It wasn't ancient history. It was still alive and tangible."

Nineteen ninety-four saw Ransom settle in as an American history teacher at the San Jacinto Christian Academy on Sixth Street—a red brick, white-steepled church and school of substantial proportions resting amid a number of former highway-side gas stations and garages that scream of Route 66's best days.

"When I realized Sixth Street was Route 66, I realized I had an opportunity to reach a whole new generation about Route 66," says Ransom. "I was enjoying my own little discovery of Route 66, and I knew that by

Curteich postcards captured the spirit of traveling and the individual characters of various places. They gave their recipients a taste of being there like no others.

teaching a class about 66, I would learn more. I thought it was something cool, and I wanted to see what the kids thought. The kids enjoyed it, and they enjoyed it for the same reasons I did. It was a history they could touch, and it was filled with people who were still alive. The idea that they would someday be able to drive on it, shop on it, and experience it was really neat for them. They couldn't do that with the Alamo. They couldn't explore with Lewis and Clark, and they couldn't fly kites with Benjamin Franklin, but they could meet the artists, take the tours led by the authors and historians of the road, and they could participate in its preservation."

As Ransom and her students realized their find, Ransom's collection began to take shape.

"As a teacher you're always showered with gifts, and a teacher collects a lot of apples. When I began teaching about Route 66, I began receiving a lot of Route 66 gifts. I would meet a lot of salesmen of Route 66 merchandise at the Big Texan, and I would talk the salesmen out of samples for the classroom—books,

maps, pieces of pavement, photos, calendars, postcards. . . . I'd have the kids pass them around so they were actually touching pieces of history. These were things they could actually see for themselves, and they could look forward to going on trips of their own someday and building their own collections. As the years progressed, and as my collection grew, the excitement among the kids grew. I think the neatest piece of memorabilia I ever brought into the classroom was the piece of the Chain of Rocks Bridge that I purchased from Jim Gilbert while on a trip to Carthage, Missouri. They reacted to this piece of the bridge just like kids in previous years had reacted to pieces of the Berlin Wall—with awe and amazement—but there was one difference: They could someday go to the Chain of Rocks Bridge and walk on it. The Berlin Wall is gone."

Ransom's classroom was a wonderland of Route 66 trinkets of all the modern varieties—some from her own collection with others as gifts from the children. Ransom's personal passion is for the Blue Whale near

Sixth-grade history teacher Becky Ransom of Amarillo, Texas, happened upon the value of Route 66 as a teaching tool while working part-time at the Big Texan Gift Shop: "I was enjoying my own little discovery of Route 66, and I knew that by teaching a class about 66, I would learn more. I thought it was something cool, and I wanted to see what the kids thought. The kids enjoyed it, and they enjoyed it for the same reasons I did. It was a history they could touch, and it was filled with people who were still alive."
Scott Piotrowski

The Class of 1999 at the San Jacinto Christian Academy in Amarillo. With Becky Ransom's collection in hand, these sixth-grade history students travel through the twentieth century on Route 66 and learn all about the places and events the road touched.

Catoosa, Oklahoma, and her end-of-unit prizes to her students always include a Blue Whale button.

"My own pictures of Route 66 had a noticeable impact because, from the kids' points of view, I was talking from my own experience and had actually been there. When the people of the road started getting involved, that had an impact because they were sending autographed books and e-mails, making personal appearances, and answering the kids' letters."

As the children became interested in the history of Route 66, Ransom began sneaking other history lessons into the mix on the unsuspecting students. Before the children realized it, their studies of Route 66 dovetailed into studies of preceding wagon trails, railroads, the Great Depression, World War II, and the presidential administrations of Roosevelt, Truman, and Eisenhower. Most important to Ransom, it brought the children's attention to their own backyard.

"It definitely tuned them in to Amarillo," Ransom says. "They were not only worried about Route 66, they were worried about other parts of town that were disappearing. There was a courthouse in town that was going to be torn down, and the kids asked their parents to help save the courthouse. They seemed to get a little more civic-minded, and I hope that continues as these kids grow up."

STEVE RIDER

Steve Rider admits that he, like most, doesn't explore his own backyard much. It's the distant, mythic lands that hold the most curiosity and become the goals to be attained. Albany, New York, in the history-rich Hudson River Valley, calls Rider a native son, and in spite of Route 66's nearest point being a 16-hour drive away from his home, Rider has become a noted 66 memorabilia collector. His Route 66 Garage has grown to be one of the collecting world's most polished Route 66 presentations.

Rider was born on Route 66's 23rd birthday—November 11, 1949—and a decade later, Rider got his first look at Route 66.

"That was in 1959. I was the youngest of three boys, and we were in a '58 Chevy Bel Air," Rider recalls. "We took U.S. 30 and U.S. 40 to California. Then we headed south. I followed along on a map, and I knew when we were on a red road we were going to make good time. The red roads were the U.S. highways, and some of the better state highways. I also

learned what a blue highway was—the well-maintained secondary roads we used to get to some destinations. We even saw some of these newfangled things called dual highways! Even at that age, I knew what Route 66 was, and I looked forward to getting on it. I knew it was *the* major road west. I knew of the *Grapes of Wrath*, and I knew the song—'. . . get your kicks . . .' and all that. This was all before the TV show. There were some things along 66 that I was pretty hepped up to see like Meteor Crater and the Painted Desert."

After seeing the Grand Canyon, the young Rider saw 66 for the first time in Flagstaff, Arizona, and shortly thereafter got his first Route 66 collectible—a piece of the meteor that formed Arizona's second most famous hole in the ground. Rider seems to recall a rubber tomahawk entering his life on this trip. With a subconscious eye to the future, Rider took a photo of a nearby sign—"Meteor City, population 2"—with the road clearly visible in the frame.

Adulthood and an education took Rider into his career where he got a bit of a reminder.

"The first teaching job I had was right on New York State Highway 66, and very often, I would see that sign on my way to the school and want to get back out there and see that road. Another thing was rediscovering

After completing a tour of Route 66, Steve Rider of Albany, New York, made a 16-hour drive from Chicago to Albany so he could tell his friends, "I was on Route 66 this morning, and I'm home tonight.
Marc Mirabile

two-lane travel, and I began traveling all over the East—a lot of the time on old U.S. 20 here in New York, which has some of the era-based trappings of 66. I love the Southwest, and I love the '50s so the desire to see Route 66 again was a natural."

Rider began riding Route 66 again in 1992, and the garage he built began to take its museum-like form.

"The garage was built in 1988 to store my Thunderbirds, and I had mixed petroliana stuff out there—pictures of cars and old gas stations I had taken," he says. "Then came the 66 stuff. The first memorabilia I bought was the 1950 National Route 66 Association brochure at an auto show flea market in 1993. Then in 1996, at Route 66 Motors near Rolla, Missouri, they had a basket of Route 66 postcards. I'm up to about 3,000 postcards now. Pretty soon, I started getting match covers

Steve Rider's museum-like Route 66 Garage—one of the most organized private collections of Mother Road memorabilia.
Marc Mirabile

Authentic marker
shields grace Rider's
Route 66 Garage.
Marc Mirabile

A treasured possession in the Steve Rider
collection is this place mat from Illinois' famous
Pig Hip Restaurant autographed by owner Ernie
Edwards, who gave Rider a long, memory-filled
conversation along with the gift. *Marc Mirabile*

Colorful postcards, matchbooks, and maps help make up the paper side of Steve Rider's collection. *Marc Mirabile*

and brochures from old businesses. By the time I made my trip in '97, I had a pretty good start on the collection, and I was looking for more—looking for pavement and relics along the road. I wound up with at least 50 pavement samples from all eight states—all from what you'd say are abandoned sections where piles of pavement were scraped away for repaving. I would never collect anything that was still in use or intact.

"The pieces that are most significant are the ones that I collected myself on-site. I spent a lot of time walking in the weeds along the road, and I found old bottles and cans from the '50s. Another neat place I stopped was in the desert near Essex, California, at the ruins of an old rest stop. I walked all around that place, and I

Among others, the Coral Court and Munger Moss Motels are represented in the Rider collection.
Marc Mirabile

pulled out some great little artifacts like a can opener, a vegetable peeler, and a bunch of bottles—most of them broken with one or two intact like a Nehi bottle and a Coke bottle. I was really wishing these things could talk about the people who left them there."

Even more urban settings have been happy hunting grounds for Rider's obsession.

"One of the places I stopped [at] in 1997 was the former site of the Coral Court Motel on the outskirts of St. Louis," he tells. "They were building condominiums on the property, and there were still vacant lots. I walked around on the lots, and there were still pieces of ceramic tile and glass lying all over the place. I have an intact glass brick, and I have a fairly large, intact, yellowish tile and a smaller dark brown tile from the trim."

Three authentic late-generation highway markers have found their homes in Rider's collection, which look at home when facing Rider's two vintage Thunderbirds.

"You just look at those 66 signs, and you just romanticize about them and what might have passed by them and what era they represent. You better believe I wish they could talk."

Rider's travels and collection will continue and grow, making for some legitimate bragging rights.

"At the end of my 1997 trip, I drove from Chicago to Albany in one shot—16 hours. I did it to say I did it, because I wanted to be able to call my friends in Albany and tell them, 'I was on Route 66 this morning, and I'm home tonight!'"

As with the many who gather Route 66's fragments, Steve Rider's collection helps preserve some of the rapidly disappearing roadside relics such as Clinton, Oklahoma's Pop Hicks' Restaurant, which burned down in 1999. *Marc Mirabile*

Automotive historians are sometimes frustrated by the notion that every car on Route 66 was a Corvette from the 1950s. Route 66 was a highway dominated by four-door sedans, station wagons, and big rigs. These cards from Meyer's collection can help the Route 66 historian get an accurate and proportionate feel for what brands and body styles really traveled 66.

INDEX